הִנְנִי

THE NEW
HEBREW THROUGH PRAYER
2

Terry Kaye

Contributing Authors:
Claudia Grossman
Lori Justice

BEHRMAN HOUSE, INC.

The publisher gratefully acknowledges the cooperation
of the following sources of photographs for this book:

Ginny Twersky cover, 9, 30, 51, 84; Terry Kaye 6, 37; Shirley Berger 19;
Gila Gevirtz 20, 42, 59, 79, 87, 94; Carlyle Teague 23, 69; Israeli Scouts 26;
Creative Image Photography 29, 72, 88; Vicki L. Weber 65; Richard Lobell 93

Book and Cover Design: Irving S. Berman
Electronic Composition and Page Production: 21st Century Publishing and Communications
Artist: Ilene Winn-Lederer

TABLE OF CONTENTS

Aleinu
V'ahavta

אָבוֹת

AVOT

1

When someone asks who you are, you might answer with your name, or with something you like to do ("I'm a ballerina!"), or even by mentioning a relationship ("I'm a big brother!").

The אָבוֹת is the first blessing of the Amidah—a group of blessings at the heart of every prayer service. It asks God to recognize us as descendants of our ancestors Abraham, Isaac, and Jacob, and it links each of us to the family of Abraham and Sarah. It asks God to watch over us, protect us, and bless us, just as God watched over our ancestors.

In the Avot we recognize that God is mighty, powerful, and awesome, but also loving and protective. You can see this balance in your everyday life, too—your mom might be strict about you doing your homework, but she can also be loving and supportive when she helps you with it and praises you when you do well.

Practice reading the אָבוֹת aloud.

1. בָּרוּךְ אַתָּה יְיָ, אֱלֹהֵינוּ וֵאלֹהֵי אֲבוֹתֵינוּ,

2. אֱלֹהֵי אַבְרָהָם, אֱלֹהֵי יִצְחָק, וֵאלֹהֵי יַעֲקֹב.

3. הָאֵל הַגָּדוֹל, הַגִּבּוֹר, וְהַנּוֹרָא, אֵל עֶלְיוֹן.

4. גּוֹמֵל חֲסָדִים טוֹבִים וְקוֹנֵה הַכֹּל, וְזוֹכֵר חַסְדֵי אָבוֹת,

5. וּמֵבִיא גוֹאֵל לִבְנֵי בְנֵיהֶם, לְמַעַן שְׁמוֹ, בְּאַהֲבָה.

6. מֶלֶךְ עוֹזֵר וּמוֹשִׁיעַ וּמָגֵן.

7. בָּרוּךְ אַתָּה יְיָ, מָגֵן אַבְרָהָם.

Praised are You, Adonai, our God and God of our fathers,
God of Abraham, God of Isaac, and God of Jacob.
The great, mighty, and awesome God, supreme God.
You do acts of loving-kindness and create everything and remember the kindnesses of the fathers,
and You will bring a redeemer to their children's children for the sake of Your name, and in love.
Ruler, Helper, Rescuer, and Shield.
Praised are You, Adonai, Shield of Abraham.

אָבוֹת וְאִמָּהוֹת

Avot Imahot

When you look at yourself, what do you see? Did you inherit blue eyes from your mom? Or a sense of humor from your grandmother? Or perhaps you're an artist just like your great-grandmother. You are descended from all of these women—and the characteristics they have passed on to you are part of your heritage.

Many congregations now include the אִמָּהוֹת in the Avot blessing. Adding the names of the Imahot links us directly to the matriarchs of the Jewish people—Sarah, Rebecca, Leah and Rachel. Just as we ask God to recognize us as descendants of the patriarchs Abraham, Isaac, and Jacob, we ask God to deal kindly with us because of the goodness of the matriarchs.

Whether the Amidah includes just the names of the Avot or also those of the Imahot, it reminds us that as Jews we have inherited God's favor because of our ancestors' goodness and faith.

Practice reading the אָבוֹת וְאִמָּהוֹת aloud.

1. בָּרוּךְ אַתָּה יְיָ, אֱלֹהֵינוּ וֵאלֹהֵי אֲבוֹתֵינוּ וְאִמּוֹתֵינוּ,

2. אֱלֹהֵי אַבְרָהָם, אֱלֹהֵי יִצְחָק, וֵאלֹהֵי יַעֲקֹב, אֱלֹהֵי שָׂרָה,

3. אֱלֹהֵי רִבְקָה, אֱלֹהֵי לֵאָה וְרָחֵל. הָאֵל הַגָּדוֹל, הַגִּבּוֹר,

4. וְהַנּוֹרָא, אֵל עֶלְיוֹן. גּוֹמֵל חֲסָדִים טוֹבִים וְקוֹנֵה הַכֹּל,

5. וְזוֹכֵר חַסְדֵי אָבוֹת וְאִמָּהוֹת, וּמֵבִיא גּוֹאֵל/גְּאֻלָּה לִבְנֵי בְנֵיהֶם,

6. לְמַעַן שְׁמוֹ, בְּאַהֲבָה. מֶלֶךְ עוֹזֵר וּמוֹשִׁיעַ וּמָגֵן.

7. בָּרוּךְ אַתָּה יְיָ, מָגֵן אַבְרָהָם וְעֶזְרַת שָׂרָה.

(margin note: Elohei Rachael v'Elohei Leah)

Praised are You, Adonai, our God and God of our fathers and mothers,
God of Abraham, God of Isaac, and God of Jacob, God of Sarah,
God of Rebecca, God of Leah and Rachel. The great, mighty, and awesome God, supreme God.
You do acts of loving-kindness and create everything and remember the kindnesses of the fathers
and mothers, and You will bring a redeemer/redemption to their children's children
for the sake of Your name, and in love. Ruler, Helper, Rescuer, and Shield.
Praised are You, Adonai, Shield of Abraham and Help of Sarah.

PRAYER VARIATIONS

Some congregations pray for God to bring a redeemer (גּוֹאֵל)—the Messiah—who will bring peace to the world, while other congregations pray for redemption (גְּאֻלָּה)—a state of peace and perfection in the world. But *all* Jews are alike in praying for a better and more peaceful world.

SEARCH AND CIRCLE

Circle the Hebrew word that means the same as the English.

fathers	אַבְרָהָם	(אָבוֹת)	אוֹר
our fathers	(אֲבוֹתֵינוּ)	אֱלֹהֵינוּ	אַתָּה
God of	יִשְׂרָאֵל	וְאָהַבְתָּ	(אֱלֹהֵי)

PRAYER DICTIONARY

אָבוֹת
fathers

אֲבוֹתֵינוּ
our fathers

אֱלֹהֵי
God of

אַבְרָהָם
Abraham

יִצְחָק
Isaac

יַעֲקֹב
Jacob

We show love and respect for our mothers, fathers, and grandparents in many ways, including by helping them with chores around the house.

NAME GAME

Connect the Hebrew and English names of the fathers.

Isaac   אַבְרָהָם

Jacob   יִצְחָק

Abraham   יַעֲקֹב

WHO'S MISSING?

Fill in the name of the missing father.

אֱלֹהֵי אַבְרָהָם, אֱלֹהֵי _יִצְחָק_ ,
וֵאלֹהֵי יַעֲקֹב.

Now write the name in English. _Issac_

6

אִמָּהוֹת

mothers

אִמוֹתֵינוּ

our mothers

אֱלֹהֵי

God of

שָׂרָה

Sarah

רִבְקָה

Rebecca

לֵאָה

Leah

רָחֵל

Rachel

SEARCH AND CIRCLE

Circle the Hebrew word that means the same as the English.

English			
mothers	הָאֲדָמָה	(אִמָּהוֹת)	אֱמֶת
our mothers	הָאָרֶץ	אֵלִיָּהוּ	(אִמוֹתֵינוּ)
God of	(אֱלֹהֵי)	אַבְרָהָם	אָרוֹן

NAME GAME

Connect the Hebrew and English names of the mothers.

Leah   שָׂרָה

Sarah   רִבְקָה

Rachel   לֵאָה

Rebecca   רָחֵל

WHO'S MISSING?

Fill in the names of the missing mothers.

אֱלֹהֵי רִבְקָה, אֱלֹהֵי ____שָׂרָה____,

לֵאָה וְ____רָחֵל____

Now write the names in English.

____Sarah____   ____Rachel____

7

IN THE SYNAGOGUE

אָבוֹת is the first blessing in a very old and very important group of blessings called the עֲמִידָה. The עֲמִידָה is the heart or center of every synagogue service.

The עֲמִידָה has many names:

- The Hebrew name עֲמִידָה means "standing." We always stand when we say the עֲמִידָה. It is as if we are standing in front of God.

- It is sometimes called the "Silent Prayer" because many people say it in a very quiet voice. They are talking privately to God.

- Another name is שְׁמוֹנֶה עֶשְׂרֵה (the Hebrew word for "eighteen"). Originally, the עֲמִידָה contained eighteen blessings. Now it consists of nineteen blessings (when it is said on a weekday) or seven blessings (when it is said on Shabbat and holidays). The first three blessings and the last three blessings of every עֲמִידָה are always the same. Only the middle section changes.

- The עֲמִידָה is so important that many congregations simply call it the "Prayer" (תְּפִלָה).

▶ אָבוֹת
גְּבוּרוֹת
קְדוּשָׁה
קְדוּשַׁת הַיּוֹם
עֲבוֹדָה
הוֹדָאָה
בִּרְכַּת שָׁלוֹם

TRUE OR FALSE

Put a ✔ next to each sentence that is true.

_✔_ The אָבוֹת refers to our relationship with our ancestors.

___ The אָבוֹת is the last part of the עֲמִידָה. Begining

_✔_ The עֲמִידָה is said at every synagogue service. nineteen-weekd

_✔_ Another name for the עֲמִידָה is שְׁמוֹנֶה עֶשְׂרֵה.

___ The עֲמִידָה always contains 18 blessings. nineteen-weekday / Seven -Shabbat & Holidays

_✔_ When we say the "Prayer," we are referring to the עֲמִידָה.

הַגָּדוֹל
the great

הַגִּבּוֹר
the mighty

וְהַנּוֹרָא
and the awesome

עֶלְיוֹן
supreme

חֲסָדִים טוֹבִים
acts of loving-kindness

מֶלֶךְ
ruler

עוֹזֵר
helper

וּמוֹשִׁיעַ
and rescuer

וּמָגֵן
and shield

GOD'S GREATNESS

אָבוֹת lists four words to describe God's greatness.

Write the English meaning for each one.

Supreme	_and The awesome_	_The mighty_	_The Great_
עֶלְיוֹן	וְהַנּוֹרָא	הַגִּבּוֹר	הַגָּדוֹל

In אָבוֹת we see four roles that God plays in the lives of the Jewish people.

Write the English meaning for each one.

and shield	_and rescuer_	_helper_	_ruler_
וּמָגֵן	וּמוֹשִׁיעַ	עוֹזֵר	מֶלֶךְ

The Amidah is also called the "Standing Prayer." When we say it, we stand respectfully before God.

Prayer Building Blocks

אֱלֹהֵי   **"God of"**

אֵל or אֱלֹהִים   means "God."

אֱלֹהֵי   means "God of."

Why do you think the word אֱלֹהֵי ("God of") is repeated before each name

in the אָבוֹת?   _In honor of GOD_

_____

הַגָּדוֹל, הַגִּבּוֹר, וְהַנּוֹרָא   **"the great, the mighty, and the awesome"**

הַגָּדוֹל   means "the great."

הַגִּבּוֹר   means "the mighty."

וְהַנּוֹרָא   means "and the awesome."

The prefix הַ means "the."

Complete the following words describing God by adding the prefix "the."

נוֹרָא הַ וְ   גִּבּוֹר הַ   גָּדוֹל הַ

Why do you think the prayer lists so many different words to describe God's

greatness?   _He is OUR GOD_

master and owner of everything

10

TORAH CONNECTION

Read this verse from the Torah (Deuteronomy 10:17).

1. כִּי יְיָ אֱלֹהֵיכֶם הוּא אֱלֹהֵי הָאֱלֹהִים

2. וַאֲדֹנֵי הָאֲדֹנִים הָאֵל הַגָּדֹל הַגִּבֹּר וְהַנּוֹרָא

Do you recognize the underlined words?

Underline the same four words as they appear in the following lines from the siddur.
(Hint: Some of the words may look slightly different.)

1. בָּרוּךְ אַתָּה יְיָ, אֱלֹהֵינוּ וֵאלֹהֵי אֲבוֹתֵינוּ,

2. אֱלֹהֵי אַבְרָהָם, אֱלֹהֵי יִצְחָק, וֵאלֹהֵי יַעֲקֹב.

3. הָאֵל הַגָּדוֹל, הַגִּבּוֹר, וְהַנּוֹרָא, אֵל עֶלְיוֹן.

4. גּוֹמֵל חֲסָדִים טוֹבִים וְקוֹנֵה הַכֹּל ...

What is the name of this prayer? _____AVOT_____

Write the English meaning of the words you underlined.

_____The Great, The mighty, and the awesome_____

Why do you think the words הָאֵל הַגָּדוֹל הַגִּבּוֹר וְהַנּוֹרָא are written in the Torah and then repeated in the עֲמִידָה?

_____

_____

עֶלְיוֹן "supreme" or "highest"

עֶלְיוֹן means "supreme" or "highest."

The word עַל means "on" or "above."

Underline the Hebrew letters that mean "above" in this word:

עֶלְיוֹן

Why do you think God is called "supreme" or "highest"? Because He is Master and owner of everything

---

חֲסָדִים טוֹבִים "acts of loving-kindness"

חֲסָדִים means "acts (of loving-kindness)."

טוֹבִים means "good."

In the phrase חֲסָדִים טוֹבִים, the word טוֹבִים helps us know how *good* the acts of loving-kindness are.

Which of the following are חֲסָדִים טוֹבִים? Circle the numbers.

1. Abraham welcomes and cares for strangers. *(circled)*

2. Haman forces the Jews to bow down to him.

3. You take home schoolwork for a sick friend. *(circled)*

4. A store owner gives employment to a needy person. *(circled)*

5. Jacob tricks his father, Isaac, into giving him Esau's blessing.

Add your own example of an act of loving-kindness.

Bringing food to someone who is ILL

12

מֶלֶךְ עוֹזֵר וּמוֹשִׁיעַ וּמָגֵן — "ruler, helper, and rescuer and shield"

מֶלֶךְ means "king, ruler."

עוֹזֵר means "helper."

וּמוֹשִׁיעַ means "and rescuer."

וּמָגֵן means "and shield."

Write the Hebrew word for "helper." _____ עוֹזֵר

Write the Hebrew word for "and rescuer." _____ וּמוֹשִׁיעַ

Circle the Hebrew word part that means "and" in these two words.

וּמוֹשִׁיעַ וּמָגֵן

Fill in the Hebrew word for "shield" in the blanks.

מֶלֶךְ עוֹזֵר וּמוֹשִׁיעַ וּ מָגֵן _____

בָּרוּךְ אַתָּה יְיָ, מָגֵן _____ אַבְרָהָם.

Why do you think God is compared to a shield?

_____

An Ethical Echo

An important part of the אָבוֹת blessing is the belief in זְכוּת אָבוֹת—"the merit of the ancestors"—which means that we are favored with God's love and care because of the goodness of our ancestors. We have inherited the gift of God's generosity, kindness, and protection because of their faith and their righteousness.

Think About This!

Do you think that זְכוּת אָבוֹת is enough by itself to grant us God's care and love, or do we also need to *earn* those rewards? What good things have you done, or would you like to do, in your life to become worthy of God's blessings and to someday make your children, grandchildren, and great-grandchildren proud?

FAMILY TREE

Abraham, Isaac, and Jacob are called the אָבוֹת ("fathers") of Judaism. Sarah, Rebecca, Leah, and Rachel are called the אִמָּהוֹת ("mothers") of Judaism. They were the first family to believe in one God.

Fill in the missing English names on our ancestors' family tree.

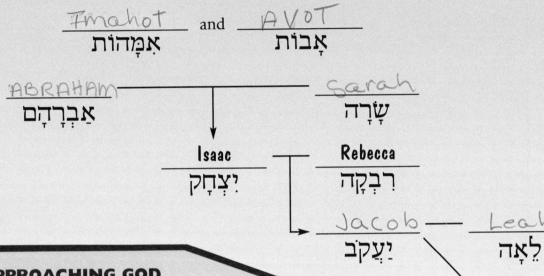

Imahot and **AVOT**
אִמָּהוֹת   אָבוֹת

ABRAHAM   **Sarah**
אַבְרָהָם   שָׂרָה

Isaac — **Rebecca**
יִצְחָק   רִבְקָה

Jacob — **Leah**
יַעֲקֹב   לֵאָה

Rachael
רָחֵל

APPROACHING GOD

When we say the עֲמִידָה we are approaching God with our prayer. It is as if we are in the presence of a king or a queen, so we behave in a special way.

In some synagogues we:
1. Stand.
2. Face toward Jerusalem.
3. Take three small steps forward before we begin.
4. Bow at the beginning of אָבוֹת and at the end of אָבוֹת.
5. Bow several more times during the עֲמִידָה.
6. Don't stop to talk while reading the prayer.
7. Take three small steps backward when we finish the prayer.

How do you think you would feel and behave in front of a king or a queen?

with respect / Honored

Who is the Ruler we are addressing in the עֲמִידָה? Write your answer in English and in Hebrew.

English: _____ Hebrew: _____

FLUENT READING

Each line below contains a word or phrase you know. Practice reading the lines.

1. עֶזְרַת אֲבוֹתֵינוּ אַתָּה הוּא מֵעוֹלָם, מָגֵן וּמוֹשִׁיעַ.

2. אֱמֶת, אֱלֹהֵי עוֹלָם מַלְכֵּנוּ, צוּר יַעֲקֹב מָגֵן יִשְׁעֵנוּ.

3. אֶת שֵׁם הָאֵל הַמֶּלֶךְ הַגָּדוֹל, הַגִּבּוֹר וְהַנּוֹרָא.

4. הָאֵל הַגָּדוֹל הַגִּבּוֹר, יְיָ צְבָאוֹת שְׁמוֹ.

5. כִּי בְשֵׁם קָדְשְׁךָ הַגָּדוֹל וְהַנּוֹרָא בָּטָחְנוּ.

6. מָגֵן אָבוֹת בִּדְבָרוֹ.

7. עַל הַתּוֹרָה וְעַל הָעֲבוֹדָה וְעַל גְּמִילוּת חֲסָדִים.

8. אָבִינוּ מַלְכֵּנוּ, עֲשֵׂה לְמַעַן שִׁמְךָ הַגָּדוֹל הַגִּבּוֹר וְהַנּוֹרָא.

9. עֹשֶׂה חֶסֶד לַאֲלָפִים.

10. וַאֲנִי, בְּרֹב חַסְדְּךָ אָבוֹא בֵיתֶךָ.

גְּבוּרוֹת

Gevurot

I f you've ever seen a lightning storm, you've witnessed God's power in nature. And if you've watched the first leaves bloom on your favorite backyard tree after a long, cold winter, you've observed God's power to give and sustain life.

The second blessing of the Amidah is called גְּבוּרוֹת ("powers"). In it, we praise God's awesome powers. These powers are evidence of God's greatness—the same greatness that gives us life and the strength to make the world a better place.

Practice reading the גְּבוּרוֹת aloud.

1. אַתָּה גִּבּוֹר לְעוֹלָם, אֲדֹנָי, מְחַיֵּה הַכֹּל/מֵתִים אַתָּה, רַב לְהוֹשִׁיעַ.

2. מְכַלְכֵּל חַיִּים בְּחֶסֶד, מְחַיֵּה הַכֹּל/מֵתִים בְּרַחֲמִים רַבִּים. סוֹמֵךְ

3. נוֹפְלִים, וְרוֹפֵא חוֹלִים, וּמַתִּיר אֲסוּרִים, וּמְקַיֵּם אֱמוּנָתוֹ לִישֵׁנֵי עָפָר.

4. מִי כָמוֹךָ, בַּעַל גְּבוּרוֹת, וּמִי דוֹמֶה לָּךְ, מֶלֶךְ מֵמִית וּמְחַיֶּה

5. וּמַצְמִיחַ יְשׁוּעָה?

6. וְנֶאֱמָן אַתָּה לְהַחֲיוֹת הַכֹּל/מֵתִים. בָּרוּךְ אַתָּה, יְיָ,

7. מְחַיֵּה הַכֹּל/הַמֵּתִים.

Reform *Orthodox*

You are eternally mighty (powerful), Adonai, You give life to all/the dead, great is Your power to save.

With kindness You sustain the living, with great compassion (mercy) give life to all/the dead. You help the falling, and heal the sick, and You free the captive, and keep faith with those who sleep in the dust.

Who is like You, God of Power, and who is comparable to You, Ruler who brings death and gives life and who is a source of salvation?

You are faithful to give life to all/the dead. Blessed are You, Adonai, who gives life to all/the dead.

PRAYER DICTIONARY

אַתָּה
you (are)

גִּבּוֹר
mighty, powerful

לְעוֹלָם
eternally

מְחַיֶּה
give life

לְהוֹשִׁיעַ
to save

חַיִּים
life, the living

בְּרַחֲמִים
with compassion, mercy

מִי כָמוֹךָ
who is like you?

WHAT'S MISSING?

Fill in the missing word(s) in each Hebrew phrase.

1. אַתָּה _____ לְעוֹלָם, אֲדֹנָי
You are eternally *mighty (powerful)*, Adonai

2. רַב _____
great is your power *to save*

3. מְכַלְכֵּל _____ בְּחֶסֶד
with kindness you sustain *life (the living)*

4. _____ , בַּעַל גְּבוּרוֹת
who is like you, God of Power

PRAYER VARIATIONS

Reform and Reconstructionist prayer books use the phrase
מְחַיֶּה כֹּל חַי and מְחַיֶּה הַכֹּל ("gives life to everything") in
the גְּבוּרוֹת. Conservative and Orthodox prayer books contain
the words מְחַיֶּה הַמֵּתִים ("revives the dead").

The concept of "reviving the dead" is called *resurrection*.
Belief in resurrection is the belief that, at some time in the
future, all those who have died will be brought back to life
by God.

Some people interpret the phrase "reviving the dead"
symbolically, and use it to refer to the cycle of nature. For
example, plants that are dormant and animals that hibernate
in the winter become active again in the spring.

Whether or not they believe in resurrection, most Jews
believe that the soul (נֶפֶשׁ) lives on forever. The soul is a part
of God in each of us.

Which version of the גְּבוּרוֹת is found in your synagogue's
prayer book?

POWERFUL WORDS

Circle the Hebrew word or phrase that means the same as the English.

who is like you?	מִי כָמוֹךָ	חֲסָדִים טוֹבִים	לְעוֹלָם וָעֶד
life, the living	אֱמֶת	זִכָּרוֹן	חַיִּים
eternally	עֶלְיוֹן	לְעוֹלָם	וְעַל
mighty, powerful	גִּבּוֹר	גּוֹמֵל	מֶלֶךְ
you (are)	אֶחָד	אַתָּה	אָבוֹת
give life	מְחַיֶּה	מָגֵן	מוֹשִׁיעַ
with compassion, mercy	וּבְרָצוֹן	בְּרַחֲמִים	בְּאַהֲבָה
to save	לְהוֹשִׁיעַ	לִיצִיאַת	לְהַדְלִיק

IT'S A MATCH!

Match the Hebrew word to its English meaning.

give life	גִּבּוֹר
life, the living	מְחַיֶּה
eternally	חַיִּים
mighty, powerful	לְעוֹלָם

THEME OF גְּבוּרוֹת

The גְּבוּרוֹת praises God's power, or ability, to:

1. create life
2. save life
3. sustain life

4. help the falling
5. heal the sick
6. free the captive

Since we are created in God's image (בְּצֶלֶם אֱלֹהִים), we have the ability to act in godly ways.

Choose 3 of God's powers from the list above, and give an example of what people can do to imitate God. Here is one example:

heal the sick—We can become doctors or nurses who work to cure illness and disease.

1. _____

2. _____

3. _____

Holding a baby can fill us with the wonder of God's creations and all the possibilities that the future can bring.

WHERE ARE WE?

Let's put the גְּבוּרוֹת in the context of a prayer service.

Every prayer service contains a version of the עֲמִידָה.
The first three and the last three blessings of every
עֲמִידָה are blessings of praise and are always the same.
Only the middle בְּרָכוֹת change.

גְּבוּרוֹת is the *second* blessing in the עֲמִידָה.

What is the name of the *first* blessing in the עֲמִידָה?
Write your answer in Hebrew and in English.

אָבוֹת
▶ גְּבוּרוֹת
קְדוּשָׁה
קְדוּשַׁת הַיּוֹם
עֲבוֹדָה
הוֹדָאָה
בִּרְכַּת שָׁלוֹם

Hebrew: _____

English: _____

Do you recall the theme or subject of the first blessing in the עֲמִידָה? Write it here.

_____

We feel God's presence in the world through acts of kindness and compassion.
The Jewish communities of France donated this ambulance to the State of Israel
to help heal the sick and save lives.

20

Prayer Building Blocks

אַתָּה גִּבּוֹר לְעוֹלָם "you are eternally mighty (powerful)"

אַתָּה means "you."

Whom are we addressing? _____

גִּבּוֹר means "mighty" or "powerful."

Write the name of the blessing you are studying. _____

Can you see the connection between the word גִּבּוֹר and the name of the blessing?

Both words mean _____.

לְעוֹלָם means "eternally" or "forever."

לְעוֹלָם וָעֶד also means "eternally" or "forever."

Draw a circle around the words לְעוֹלָם וָעֶד or לְעוֹלָם wherever they appear below.

Practice reading the sentences aloud.

1. וְלֹא נֵבוֹשׁ לְעוֹלָם וָעֶד.

2. בָּרוּךְ יְיָ הַמְבֹרָךְ לְעוֹלָם וָעֶד.

3. דָּבָר טוֹב וְקַיָּם לְעוֹלָם וָעֶד.

4. שָׁלוֹם רָב עַל־יִשְׂרָאֵל עַמְּךָ תָּשִׂים לְעֹלָם.

5. בֵּינִי וּבֵין בְּנֵי יִשְׂרָאֵל אוֹת הִיא לְעוֹלָם.

6. אֵל חַי וְקַיָּם, תָּמִיד יִמְלֹךְ עָלֵינוּ לְעוֹלָם וָעֶד.

21

מְחַיֶּה "give life"

מְחַיֶּה means "give life."

The root of מְחַיֶּה is חיה.

The root חיה tells us that "life" is part of a word's meaning.

In each sentence below circle the word(s) with the root חיה.

(Remember: Sometimes a root letter is missing from a word.)

Practice reading the sentences aloud.

1. עַם יִשְׂרָאֵל חַי. עוֹד אָבִינוּ חַי.

2. כִּי הֵם חַיֵּינוּ וְאֹרֶךְ יָמֵינוּ.

3. בָּרוּךְ אַתָּה, יְיָ אֱלֹהֵינוּ, מֶלֶךְ הָעוֹלָם, אֲשֶׁר נָתַן־לָנוּ תּוֹרַת אֱמֶת וְחַיֵּי עוֹלָם נָטַע בְּתוֹכֵנוּ.

4. דָּוִד מֶלֶךְ יִשְׂרָאֵל חַי וְקַיָּם.

5. וְתִתֶּן לָנוּ חַיִּים אֲרֻכִים, חַיִּים שֶׁל שָׁלוֹם, חַיִּים שֶׁל טוֹבָה, חַיִּים שֶׁל בְּרָכָה.

6. וְיַמְלִיךְ מַלְכוּתֵהּ בְּחַיֵּיכוֹן וּבְיוֹמֵיכוֹן וּבְחַיֵּי דְכָל־בֵּית יִשְׂרָאֵל.

Look back at the גְּבוּרוֹת blessing on page 16. Circle all the words with the root חיה. How many words did you circle? _____

מְכַלְכֵּל חַיִּים בְּחֶסֶד "with kindness you sustain the living"

חַיִּים means "living" or "life."

Write the root of חַיִּים. ____ ____ ____

בְּחֶסֶד means "with kindness."

בְּ means _____.

חֶסֶד means _____.

22

"LIVELY" TIDBITS

- Did you ever see grownups clink glasses and toast each other with the word "לְחַיִּים"—"To Life!"?

- Is there someone in your class wearing a חַי necklace? We know that חַי means "life."

- Did you know that each Hebrew letter also has a numerical value? There's even a system—called *gematria*—of interpreting a Hebrew word by adding up the value of its letters. For example, the letter ח has the value 8 and the letter י has the value 10. Together they add up to 18—and they spell the word חַי! That's why we often give monetary gifts at Jewish celebrations in multiples of $18.

  Why do you think it is appropriate to give gifts in multiples of $18?

  _____

  _____

People often give gifts in multiples of $18 in celebration of weddings and other lifecycle events.

בְּרַחֲמִים רַבִּים "with great compassion"

בְּרַחֲמִים means "with compassion" or "with mercy."

בְּ means _____.

רַחֲמִים means _____.

The root of בְּרַחֲמִים is רחם.

The root רחם tells us that "compassion" or "mercy" is part of a word's meaning.

God is sometimes referred to as אֵל מָלֵא רַחֲמִים.

Fill in the missing word in the English translation of that phrase.

God full of _____.

Here are three other names by which God is known. Circle the root letters רחם in each phrase.

אַב הָרַחֲמִים	אֵל חַנּוּן וְרַחוּם	הָרַחֲמָן
Merciful Parent	Gracious and Compassionate God	The Merciful One

The Talmud tells us that if we expect compassion from God, we should show compassion to others. Describe one way you can show compassion to others.

_____

_____

מִי כָמוֹךָ "who is like you?"

מִי כָמוֹךָ means "who is like you."

מִי means _____ .

כָמוֹךָ means _____ .

כָמוֹ means "like."

ךָ at the end of a word means _____ .

Circle כָמוֹךָ or כָמֹכָה in each line below. Then read each line.

1. אֵין כָּמוֹךָ בָאֱלֹהִים, אֲדֹנָי, וְאֵין כְּמַעֲשֶׂיךָ.

2. מִי־כָמֹכָה בָּאֵלִם, יְיָ?

3. מִי כָמֹכָה, נֶאְדָּר בַּקֹּדֶשׁ.

CHALLENGE QUESTION:

Do you remember the prayer that begins on line 2 above? When did the children of Israel first sing these words?

_____

_____

An Ethical Echo

Just as our tradition teaches that God heals the sick (רוֹפֵא חוֹלִים), so also we can help a sick person feel better. For example, we can visit, a mitzvah known as בִּקוּר חוֹלִים. Sharing time with someone who is ill can put that person in a happier mood. While doctors can help cure someone physically, the Bible teaches us—and modern science shows—that lifting the spirits of the ill can ease and speed their recovery.

Think About This!

Maybe the last time you were sick your best friend stopped by to tell you a joke, or your little sister made you a cute drawing. What else can you do to brighten the day of someone who is feeling poorly? What should you avoid doing or saying?

WHO'S YOUR HERO?

The word גִּבּוֹר means "mighty," "powerful," or "hero." A hero is somebody who does something brave, like climbing Mt. Everest, or who helps make the world a better place, like a doctor who discovers the cure for a disease. You too can be a hero by doing something brave or by helping others.

1. Name a hero from Jewish history who acted bravely *and* helped the Jewish people. Describe what he or she did.

   _____

   _____

   _____

2. Describe something brave that *you* have done. Did it help to make your home, school, or even the world a better place? Explain your answer.

   _____

   _____

   _____

A hero isn't just someone who climbs mountains or saves lives. For example, Israeli scouts such as these are heroes when they help feed those in need.

Some congregations include בִּרְכַּת כֹּהֲנִים ("the Priestly Blessing") as part of the Amidah. These words were recited by the כֹּהֲנִים (priests) who served in the ancient Temple about 2,000 years ago. The prayer asks God to bless us, to be gracious to us, and to give us peace.

Practice reading בִּרְכַּת כֹּהֲנִים below.

1. יְבָרֶכְךָ יְיָ וְיִשְׁמְרֶךָ.

2. יָאֵר יְיָ פָּנָיו אֵלֶיךָ וִיחֻנֶּךָּ.

3. יִשָּׂא יְיָ פָּנָיו אֵלֶיךָ וְיָשֵׂם לְךָ שָׁלוֹם.

May God bless you and keep you.
May God's face shine upon you and be gracious to you.
May God's face be lifted to you and may God grant you peace.

Some parents bless their children with these words on Friday evenings when they are together at the Shabbat dinner table. Why do you think it is especially appropriate for parents to say these words to their children?

_____

_____

קְדוּשָׁה

Kedushah

⬥ **3**

Have you ever imagined that you were someone else? Perhaps you had the role of a princess in a school play and you spoke and walked regally. Or maybe you and your buddies pretended to be pro-basketball stars. The קְדוּשָׁה, the third blessing in the Amidah, helps us stretch our imaginations so we can picture angels as they praise God.

The Torah tells us in the Book of Isaiah that winged angels praised God with the words of the Kedushah (*kadosh, kadosh, kadosh*). We are like angels when we say these words—we rise up on our toes three times and we imagine that we are elevating ourselves in the same way that the angels are elevated in God's eyes. *Kedushah* means "holy," and in this—the central blessing in the Amidah—we express our awe at God's holiness.

When we say these words, we try to focus on being kinder and more patient, more helpful and more thoughtful. In this way, the Kedushah helps us concentrate on becoming better people.

Practice reading these excerpts from the קְדוּשָׁה aloud.

1. נְקַדֵּשׁ אֶת שִׁמְךָ בָּעוֹלָם, כְּשֵׁם שֶׁמַּקְדִּישִׁים אוֹתוֹ בִּשְׁמֵי מָרוֹם,

2. כַּכָּתוּב עַל יַד נְבִיאֶךָ: וְקָרָא זֶה אֶל־זֶה וְאָמַר:

3. קָדוֹשׁ, קָדוֹשׁ, קָדוֹשׁ יְיָ צְבָאוֹת, מְלֹא כָל־הָאָרֶץ כְּבוֹדוֹ.

4. בָּרוּךְ כְּבוֹד־יְיָ מִמְּקוֹמוֹ.

5. יִמְלֹךְ יְיָ לְעוֹלָם, אֱלֹהַיִךְ צִיּוֹן, לְדֹר וָדֹר. הַלְלוּיָהּ!

6. לְדוֹר וָדוֹר נַגִּיד גָּדְלֶךָ, וּלְנֵצַח נְצָחִים קְדֻשָּׁתְךָ נַקְדִּישׁ.

7. וְשִׁבְחֲךָ, אֱלֹהֵינוּ, מִפִּינוּ לֹא יָמוּשׁ לְעוֹלָם וָעֶד.

8. בָּרוּךְ אַתָּה, יְיָ, הָאֵל הַקָּדוֹשׁ.

Let us sanctify Your name in the world, as they sanctify it in the highest heavens,
as it is written by Your prophet, and one called to another and said:

"Holy, Holy, Holy is Adonai of the heavenly legions, the whole earth is full of God's glory."

Praised is the glory of God from God's heavenly place.

Adonai will rule forever; your God, O Zion, from generation to generation. Halleluyah!
From generation to generation we will tell of Your greatness, and for all eternity we will proclaim Your holiness. And our praise of You, O God, will not depart from our mouths forever and ever.
Praised are You, Adonai, the holy God.

נְקַדֵּשׁ
let us sanctify

שִׁמְךָ
your name

כְּבוֹדוֹ
God's glory

יִמְלֹךְ
will rule

לְדוֹר וָדוֹר
from generation
to generation

נַגִּיד
we will tell

גָּדְלֶךָ
your greatness

RECOGNIZE THE WORD

On the right are words from the קְדוּשָׁה. On the left are words you already know. Draw lines to connect the related words.

(Hint: look for common roots.)

Then write the English meaning of the Hebrew word from the קְדוּשָׁה on the line next to the number.

הַגָּדוֹל	נְקַדֵּשׁ	1. _____
הַגָּדָה	יִמְלֹךְ	2. _____
כָּבוֹד	גָּדְלֶךָ	3. _____
מֶלֶךְ	שִׁמְךָ	4. _____
קָדוֹשׁ	כְּבוֹדוֹ	5. _____
שֵׁם	נַגִּיד	6. _____

The words of the Kedushah help us focus on becoming kinder and more patient.

29

| אָבוֹת |
| גְּבוּרוֹת |
| ▶ קְדוּשָׁה |
| קְדוּשַׁת הַיּוֹם |
| עֲבוֹדָה |
| הוֹדָאָה |
| בִּרְכַּת שָׁלוֹם |

AN IMPORTANT PRAYER

The קְדוּשָׁה is the third blessing of the עֲמִידָה. Because the קְדוּשָׁה declares that God is holy, we try to concentrate very hard as we say it. The שְׁמַע is another example of a prayer in which we concentrate very hard. Many people recite the שְׁמַע with their eyes closed so they can focus on its words.

DID YOU KNOW?

Our tradition teaches us that when we recite the קְדוּשָׁה we echo the angels who sing of God's glory and holiness. Just as angels might approach God with great respect, so we do the same as we say the קְדוּשָׁה.

How do we show our respect for God?

1. We say the קְדוּשָׁה only in a group of ten Jewish adults (a minyan).
2. We stand tall and straight, feet together.
3. We don't talk to our friends or leave the sanctuary.

What does this tell us about the importance of the קְדוּשָׁה?

_____

Describe another occasion when you might show someone great respect.

_____

A scribe shows great respect for the Torah by carefully repairing it.

30

Prayer Building Blocks

נְקַדֵּשׁ אֶת שִׁמְךָ בָּעוֹלָם "let us sanctify your name in the world"

נְקַדֵּשׁ means "let us sanctify."

Another way of saying "sanctify" is "make holy."

נְקַדֵּשׁ is built on the root קדשׁ.

קדשׁ tells us that "holy" is part of a word's meaning.

Write the root. _____ _____ _____

What does it mean? _____

- -

שִׁמְךָ means "your name."

שֵׁם means _____.

ךָ at the end of a word means _____.

Whose name are we sanctifying? _____

- -

בָּעוֹלָם means "in the world."

בָּ means _____.

עוֹלָם means _____.

- -

Look back at the קְדוּשָׁה on page 28. Circle all the words with the root קדשׁ, then write them on the lines below.

4. _____   1. _____

5. _____   2. _____

6. _____   3. _____

31

FROM THE SOURCES

At the heart of the קְדוּשָׁה are three verses that come from different places in the תַּנַ"ךְ (Bible).

Practice reading the three verses that come from the תַּנַ"ךְ.

1. קָדוֹשׁ, קָדוֹשׁ, קָדוֹשׁ יְיָ צְבָאוֹת, מְלֹא כָל־הָאָרֶץ כְּבוֹדוֹ.

2. בָּרוּךְ כְּבוֹד־יְיָ מִמְּקוֹמוֹ.

3. יִמְלֹךְ יְיָ לְעוֹלָם, אֱלֹהַיִךְ צִיּוֹן, לְדֹר וָדֹר. הַלְלוּיָהּ!

The first of these verses was spoken by the prophet Isaiah as he described a beautiful and mystical vision of God sitting on the Divine Throne surrounded by angels. As the angels moved their wings, they called to one another and said:

קָדוֹשׁ, קָדוֹשׁ, קָדוֹשׁ יְיָ צְבָאוֹת, מְלֹא כָל־הָאָרֶץ כְּבוֹדוֹ.

Holy, Holy, Holy is Adonai of the heavenly legions, the whole earth is full of God's glory.
(Isaiah 6:3)

In many congregations, as we recite Isaiah's words, קָדוֹשׁ, קָדוֹשׁ, קָדוֹשׁ, we rise up on our toes three times to symbolize the fluttering wings of the angels the prophet saw in his vision, and to represent the uplifting of the spirit.

Rising up on our toes is a physical way of trying to come closer to God. Can you think of another, nonphysical way you might come closer to God?

_____

_____

מְלֹא כָל־הָאָרֶץ כְּבוֹדוֹ — "the whole earth is full of God's glory"

הָאָרֶץ means "the earth."

הָ means _____.

אָרֶץ means _____.

Circle הָאָרֶץ in the following sentence from the Torah. This sentence tells us that God created the heavens and the earth in six days and on the seventh day God rested.

כִּי שֵׁשֶׁת יָמִים עָשָׂה יְיָ אֶת־הַשָּׁמַיִם וְאֶת־הָאָרֶץ,
וּבַיּוֹם הַשְּׁבִיעִי שָׁבַת וַיִּנָּפַשׁ.

What is the name of the seventh day, on which God rested? _____

- -

כְּבוֹדוֹ literally means "his glory."

כָּבוֹד means "glory."

וֹ is an ending that means "his."

As God is neither male nor female, we translate כְּבוֹדוֹ as "God's glory."

Look back at the קְדוּשָׁה on page 28. Write the numbers of the two lines that have to do with כָּבוֹד—God's glory. _____ _____

יִמְלֹךְ יְיָ לְעוֹלָם — "Adonai will rule forever"

יִמְלֹךְ means "will rule."

The root of יִמְלֹךְ is מלכ. (כ and ךְ are family letters.)

What does this root mean? _____

י at the beginning of a verb often indicates that the action will take place in the future.

לְדוֹר וָדוֹר נַגִּיד גָּדְלֶךָ

"from generation to generation we will tell of your greatness"

דוֹר means "generation."

לְדוֹר וָדוֹר is a phrase meaning "from generation to generation."

Explain in your own words the phrase "from generation to generation."

_____

Read this sentence from the Haggadah. Circle the Hebrew phrase that means "in every generation."

בְּכָל דוֹר וָדוֹר חַיָּב אָדָם לִרְאוֹת אֶת־עַצְמוֹ כְּאִלּוּ הוּא יָצָא מִמִּצְרָיִם.

In every generation, each of us should feel as though we ourselves had gone forth from Egypt.

נַגִּיד means "we will tell" or "we will relate."

You know the word הַגָּדָה. Can you see the connection between נַגִּיד and הַגָּדָה?

On which holiday do we use a הַגָּדָה? _____

הַגָּדָה literally means "telling" or "relating." What do we tell or relate on this holiday?

_____

גָּדְלֶךָ means "your greatness."

Write the Hebrew word for "great" or "big." _____

What does the ending ךָ mean? _____

Whose greatness will we relate or tell? Write your answer in Hebrew.

_____

FLUENT READING

On Shabbat there is a single middle blessing in the עֲמִידָה. This blessing praises and thanks God for creation and for מְנוּחָה, "rest," on Shabbat.

Practice reading the special Shabbat blessing in the קְדוּשַׁת הַיּוֹם—עֲמִידָה.

1. אֱלֹהֵינוּ וֵאלֹהֵי אֲבוֹתֵינוּ/וְאִמּוֹתֵינוּ, רְצֵה בִמְנוּחָתֵנוּ.

2. קַדְּשֵׁנוּ בְּמִצְוֹתֶיךָ וְתֵן חֶלְקֵנוּ בְּתוֹרָתֶךָ,

3. שַׂבְּעֵנוּ מִטּוּבֶךָ וְשַׂמְּחֵנוּ בִּישׁוּעָתֶךָ.

4. וְטַהֵר לִבֵּנוּ לְעָבְדְּךָ בֶּאֱמֶת.

5. וְהַנְחִילֵנוּ, יְיָ אֱלֹהֵינוּ, בְּאַהֲבָה וּבְרָצוֹן שַׁבַּת קָדְשֶׁךָ

6. וְיָנוּחוּ בָהּ יִשְׂרָאֵל מְקַדְּשֵׁי שְׁמֶךָ.

7. בָּרוּךְ אַתָּה יְיָ, מְקַדֵּשׁ הַשַּׁבָּת.

Underline the three words in the lines above that tell you this is a blessing.

Write the words here. _____

Circle the Hebrew word for Shabbat each time it appears in קְדוּשַׁת הַיּוֹם.

How many times did you circle this word? _____

PRAYER VARIATIONS

Many congregations include the אִמָּהוֹת when recalling the אָבוֹת. In this way, they also link their prayers to the matriarchs of the Jewish people—Sarah, Rebecca, Leah and Rachel.

How many times in a day do you say "thank you"? Probably more than you can count. You might thank your best friend for bringing his soccer ball to the game. Or maybe your sister agrees to let you borrow her sweater for the dance and you give her a hug of thanks. Not only are you thanking them, but you are also recognizing and acknowledging their kindness.

The הוֹדָאָה ("thanksgiving") blessing is the next-to-last blessing of the Amidah. In it, we thank God for our many blessings, and we recognize and acknowledge that God is One alone in creating and making possible life's goodness. Because we are expressing our gratitude to God, in many congregations we bow respectfully both at the start and at the end of the Hoda'ah blessing.

Practice reading these excerpts from the הוֹדָאָה aloud.

1. מוֹדִים אֲנַחְנוּ לָךְ, שָׁאַתָּה הוּא יְיָ אֱלֹהֵינוּ וֵאלֹהֵי אֲבוֹתֵינוּ/וְאִמוֹתֵינוּ

2. לְעוֹלָם וָעֶד. צוּר חַיֵּינוּ, מָגֵן יִשְׁעֵנוּ, אַתָּה הוּא לְדוֹר וָדוֹר.

3. נוֹדֶה לְךָ וּנְסַפֵּר תְּהִלָּתֶךָ...

4. וְעַל כֻּלָּם יִתְבָּרַךְ וְיִתְרוֹמַם שִׁמְךָ, מַלְכֵּנוּ, תָּמִיד לְעוֹלָם וָעֶד.

5. וְכֹל הַחַיִּים יוֹדוּךָ סֶלָה, וִיהַלְלוּ אֶת שִׁמְךָ בֶּאֱמֶת,

6. הָאֵל יְשׁוּעָתֵנוּ וְעֶזְרָתֵנוּ סֶלָה.

7. בָּרוּךְ אַתָּה, יְיָ, הַטּוֹב שִׁמְךָ וּלְךָ נָאֶה לְהוֹדוֹת.

*We give thanks to You, that You are Adonai our God and the God of our fathers/and mothers
forever and ever. You are the Rock of our lives, the Shield who saves us, from generation to generation.
We will give thanks to You and tell of Your praises . . .*

And for all this Your name will be praised and exalted, our Ruler, always and forever.

*And all living things will acknowledge and praise Your name in truth,
the God who is our Rescuer and our Helper.
Praised are You, Adonai, whose name is good and to whom we give thanks.*

מוֹדִים

thank, give thanks

אֲנַחְנוּ

we

נוֹדֶה

we will thank,
give thanks

תְּהִלָּתֶךָ

your praises

וִיהַלְלוּ

(they) will praise

שְׁמֶךָ

your name

בֶּאֱמֶת

in truth

לְהוֹדוֹת

to thank

FAMILY WORDS

1. Three words in the Prayer Dictionary are related to "thanks."

   Connect the Hebrew word to the correct English.

to thank	נוֹדֶה
thank, give thanks	לְהוֹדוֹת
we will thank, give thanks	מוֹדִים

2. Two words in the Prayer Dictionary are related to "praise."

   Connect the Hebrew word to the matching English.

   | your praises | וִיהַלְלוּ |
   | (they) will praise | תְּהִלָּתֶךָ |

Public acknowledgment and thanks for a job well done make teacher *and* student feel good.

37

Prayer Building Blocks

מוֹדִים אֲנַחְנוּ לָךְ "we give thanks to you"

מוֹדִים means "thank" or "give thanks."

Do you know the word תּוֹדָה? It means "thank you." Perhaps you have heard someone say תּוֹדָה רַבָּה ("thank you very much").

The next time someone is helpful to you, try saying תּוֹדָה רַבָּה.

Practice reading the prayer we say when we wake up in the morning.

A boy or a man says: מוֹדֶה אֲנִי לְפָנֶיךָ, מֶלֶךְ חַי וְקַיָם.

A girl or a woman says: מוֹדָה אֲנִי לְפָנֶיךָ, מֶלֶךְ חַי וְקַיָם.

Circle the words in the lines above that mean "thank."
(Did you notice that the form of the verb is different for a boy and for a girl?)

Why do you think we thank God when we wake up in the morning?

_____

_____

READING PRACTICE

אֲנַחְנוּ means "we."

In each prayer excerpt below, circle the word that means "we."

Practice reading the sentences aloud.

1. עַל־הַכֹּל, יְיָ אֱלֹהֵינוּ, אֲנַחְנוּ מוֹדִים לָךְ, וּמְבָרְכִים אֹתָךְ.

2. וַאֲנַחְנוּ נְבָרֵךְ יָהּ מֵעַתָּה וְעַד־עוֹלָם. הַלְלוּיָהּ.

3. וַאֲנַחְנוּ כּוֹרְעִים וּמִשְׁתַּחֲוִים וּמוֹדִים.

THE ROCKS IN YOUR LIFE

צוּר means "rock."

Who is the "rock" in the הוֹדָאָה? _____

Who are the "rocks" in your life? List them and explain why you included each one on the list.

<table>
<tr><td colspan="2"><u>MY "ROCKS"</u></td><td><u>REASON</u></td></tr>
<tr><td>1.</td><td>_____</td><td>_____</td></tr>
<tr><td>2.</td><td>_____</td><td>_____</td></tr>
<tr><td>3.</td><td>_____</td><td>_____</td></tr>
<tr><td>4.</td><td>_____</td><td>_____</td></tr>
<tr><td>5.</td><td>**Adonai**</td><td>_____</td></tr>
</table>

What are the common characteristics of all the "rocks" on your list?

_____

_____

נוֹדֶה לְךָ "we will give thanks to you"

נוֹדֶה means "we will give thanks."

לְךָ means "to you."

לְ means _____ .

ךָ means _____ .

To whom will we give thanks? _____

39

וּנְסַפֵּר תְּהִלָּתֶךְ **"and we will tell of your praises"**

תְּהִלָּתֶךְ means "your praises."

Whose praises will we tell of? _____

The root of תְּהִלָּתֶךְ is הלל.

The root הלל tell us that "praise" is part of a word's meaning.

READING PRACTICE

In each sentence below circle the word(s) built on the root הלל.

Practice reading each sentence aloud.

1. יְהַלְלוּ אֶת־שֵׁם יְיָ כִּי נִשְׂגָּב שְׁמוֹ לְבַדּוֹ.

2. וְיִתְהַדָּר וְיִתְעַלֶּה, וְיִתְהַלַּל שְׁמֵהּ דְּקֻדְשָׁא, בְּרִיךְ הוּא.

3. הַלְלוּיָהּ. הַלְלוּ אֶת־שֵׁם יְיָ.

4. הוֹדוּ עַל אֶרֶץ וְשָׁמָיִם, וַיָּרֶם קֶרֶן לְעַמּוֹ תְּהִלָּה לְכָל חֲסִידָיו לִבְנֵי יִשְׂרָאֵל עַם קְרֹבוֹ הַלְלוּיָהּ.

5. וְכֹל הַחַיִּים יוֹדוּךָ סֶּלָה, וִיהַלְלוּ אֶת שִׁמְךָ בֶּאֱמֶת.

Write the root that tell us that "praise" is part of a word's meaning.

_____ _____ _____

DID YOU KNOW? -

Some prayers are said only on holidays and special occasions. Hallel (Hymns of Praise) is a group of six psalms recited on Pesaḥ, Shavuot, and Sukkot (the three Pilgrimage Festivals), Ḥanukkah, Rosh Ḥodesh (the New Month), Yom Ha'atzmaut, and Yom Yerushalayim. Our tradition teaches that it was King David who wrote the joyful praise of God expressed in Hallel.

40

וִיהַלְלוּ אֶת שִׁמְךָ בֶּאֱמֶת "and will praise your name in truth"

וִיהַלְלוּ means "and will praise."

Write the root of וִיהַלְלוּ. ____ ____ ____

This root means _____.

שִׁמְךָ means "your name."

שֵׁם means _____.

ךָ is a suffix meaning _____.

To whose name are we referring? _____.

בֶּאֱמֶת means "in truth."

Circle the word part that means "in." בֶּאֱמֶת

אֱמֶת means _____.

Why do you think it is necessary to add the words "in truth" to the phrase "and will praise your name"?

_____

_____

READING PRACTICE

Circle the word אֱמֶת in each sentence below.

Practice reading the sentences aloud.

1. בָּרוּךְ אַתָּה, יְיָ אֱלֹהֵינוּ, מֶלֶךְ הָעוֹלָם, אֲשֶׁר בָּחַר
בִּנְבִיאִים טוֹבִים וְרָצָה בְדִבְרֵיהֶם הַנֶּאֱמָרִים בֶּאֱמֶת.

2. הָאֵל הַנֶּאֱמָן, הָאוֹמֵר וְעוֹשֶׂה, הַמְדַבֵּר וּמְקַיֵּם,
שֶׁכָּל־דְּבָרָיו אֱמֶת וָצֶדֶק.

3. עַל־שְׁלֹשָׁה דְבָרִים הָעוֹלָם קַיָּם: עַל־הָאֱמֶת וְעַל־הַדִּין
וְעַל־הַשָּׁלוֹם.

4. בָּרוּךְ אַתָּה, יְיָ אֱלֹהֵינוּ, מֶלֶךְ הָעוֹלָם, אֲשֶׁר נָתַן לָנוּ
תּוֹרַת אֱמֶת וְחַיֵּי עוֹלָם נָטַע בְּתוֹכֵנוּ.

41

SAYING "THANK YOU"

In the הוֹדָאָה prayer you have learned many forms of the word "thank." We thank God *and* acknowledge God's goodness.

In each sentence below, circle the word(s) that mean(s) "thank."

1. מוֹדִים אֲנַחְנוּ לָךְ, שָׁאַתָּה הוּא יְיָ אֱלֹהֵינוּ.

2. נוֹדֶה לֵאלֹהֵינוּ. נוֹדֶה לַאדוֹנֵינוּ. נוֹדֶה לְמַלְכֵּנוּ. נוֹדֶה לְמוֹשִׁיעֵנוּ.

3. בָּרוּךְ אַתָּה, יְיָ, הַטּוֹב שִׁמְךָ וּלְךָ נָאֶה לְהוֹדוֹת.

4. וַאֲנַחְנוּ כּוֹרְעִים וּמִשְׁתַּחֲוִים וּמוֹדִים לִפְנֵי מֶלֶךְ מַלְכֵי הַמְּלָכִים, הַקָּדוֹשׁ בָּרוּךְ הוּא.

5. טוֹב לְהֹדוֹת לַיְיָ וּלְזַמֵּר לְשִׁמְךָ עֶלְיוֹן.

6. מוֹדֶה אֲנִי לְפָנֶיךָ מֶלֶךְ חַי וְקַיָּם.

7. נוֹדֶה לְךָ וּנְסַפֵּר תְּהִלָּתֶךָ.

8. וְעַל הַכֹּל יְיָ אֱלֹהֵינוּ, אֲנַחְנוּ מוֹדִים לָךְ, וּמְבָרְכִים אוֹתָךְ.

Which of the lines above appear in the הוֹדָאָה?

Write the numbers. #_____   #_____   #_____

Which of nature's gifts are *you* thankful for?

WHERE ARE WE?

In the weekday Amidah there are nineteen blessings. The הוֹדָאָה is the eighteenth—the next-to-last—blessing.

In the Shabbat Morning Amidah there are seven blessings. The הוֹדָאָה is the sixth—also the next-to-last—blessing.

אָבוֹת
גְּבוּרוֹת
קְדוּשָׁה
קְדוּשַׁת הַיּוֹם
עֲבוֹדָה
▶ הוֹדָאָה
בִּרְכַּת שָׁלוֹם

THEME OF THE PRAYER

The theme of thanksgiving is one of the oldest in our prayers. In the הוֹדָאָה we thank God for four things:

1. Our lives

2. Our souls

3. Miracles in the world around us

4. Wonders and great gifts in the evening, in the morning, and at noon.

Give one example of a miracle or wonder in the world around you.

_____

Give one example of a miracle or wonder in your own life.

_____

DID YOU KNOW?

There are two ways to translate the Hebrew phrase מוֹדִים אֲנַחְנוּ לָךְ.

1. We thank You, God

2. We acknowledge You, God

Are thanking and acknowledging the same thing? Can you do one without the other?

_____

_____

YOUR PERSONAL THANKS

When you are grateful for something, you can *say* thank you ("Thanks for helping me fix my computer") or you can *show* your thanks (by doing a favor in return).

Name one thing for which you are grateful to God.

_____

The הוֹדָאָה prayer is a way to *say* thank you to God.

Now list 3 things you can do to *show* your thanks to God.

1. _____

2. _____

3. _____

Name one thing for which you are grateful to another person.

_____

Now list 3 things you can do to *show* your thanks to that person.

1. _____

2. _____

3. _____

What is the difference between the way you thank God and the way you thank other people?

FLUENT READING

Practice reading the complete הוֹדָאָה.

1. מוֹדִים אֲנַחְנוּ לָךְ, שָׁאַתָּה הוּא יְיָ אֱלֹהֵינוּ וֵאלֹהֵי אֲבוֹתֵינוּ/וְאִמוֹתֵינוּ

2. לְעוֹלָם וָעֶד. צוּר חַיֵּינוּ, מָגֵן יִשְׁעֵנוּ, אַתָּה הוּא לְדוֹר וָדוֹר.

3. נוֹדֶה לְךָ וּנְסַפֵּר תְּהִלָּתֶךָ, עַל־חַיֵּינוּ הַמְּסוּרִים בְּיָדֶךָ, וְעַל-

4. נִשְׁמוֹתֵינוּ הַפְּקוּדוֹת לָךְ, וְעַל־נִסֶּיךָ שֶׁבְּכָל־יוֹם עִמָּנוּ, וְעַל-

5. נִפְלְאוֹתֶיךָ וְטוֹבוֹתֶיךָ שֶׁבְּכָל־עֵת, עֶרֶב וָבֹקֶר וְצָהֳרָיִם. הַטּוֹב:

6. כִּי לֹא־כָלוּ רַחֲמֶיךָ, וְהַמְרַחֵם: כִּי־לֹא תַמּוּ חֲסָדֶיךָ,

7. מֵעוֹלָם קִוִּינוּ לָךְ.

8. וְעַל כֻּלָּם יִתְבָּרַךְ וְיִתְרוֹמַם שִׁמְךָ, מַלְכֵּנוּ, תָּמִיד לְעוֹלָם וָעֶד.

9. וְכֹל הַחַיִּים יוֹדוּךָ סֶּלָה, וִיהַלְלוּ אֶת שִׁמְךָ בֶּאֱמֶת,

10. הָאֵל יְשׁוּעָתֵנוּ וְעֶזְרָתֵנוּ סֶלָה.

11. בָּרוּךְ אַתָּה, יְיָ, הַטּוֹב שִׁמְךָ וּלְךָ נָאֶה לְהוֹדוֹת.

בִּרְכַּת שָׁלוֹם

שָׁלוֹם רָב

If you've ever made a wish while blowing away a fuzzy dandelion or throwing pennies in a fountain, you know that there are many things you can wish for. But if you had just one wish, what would it be? Maybe you'd wish for a puppy. Or maybe you'd wish you could be the star of your soccer team. Or maybe you'd even wish you were taller or had curly hair or knew how to play a musical instrument.

When the Jewish people make a wish as a community, it is a wish for peace. The idea of peace is so important to the Jews that the final blessing of the Amidah is a prayer for peace—בִּרְכַּת שָׁלוֹם.

During the evening service, this blessing begins with the words שָׁלוֹם רָב ("great peace"). In it, we ask God for peace in the world at all times. In the morning, we recite the same blessing, but it begins with a passage called שִׁים שָׁלוֹם ("grant peace"), which you will study later in this chapter.

Practice reading שָׁלוֹם רָב aloud.

1. שָׁלוֹם רָב עַל־יִשְׂרָאֵל עַמְּךָ תָּשִׂים לְעוֹלָם כִּי אַתָּה הוּא
2. מֶלֶךְ אָדוֹן לְכָל־הַשָּׁלוֹם. וְטוֹב בְּעֵינֶיךָ לְבָרֵךְ אֶת־עַמְּךָ
3. יִשְׂרָאֵל (וְאֶת־כָּל־הָעַמִּים) בְּכָל־עֵת וּבְכָל־שָׁעָה בִּשְׁלוֹמֶךָ.
4. בָּרוּךְ אַתָּה, יְיָ, הַמְבָרֵךְ אֶת־עַמּוֹ יִשְׂרָאֵל בַּשָּׁלוֹם.

May You grant great peace upon Israel Your people forever, for You are the Ruler,
Sovereign of all peace. And may it be good in Your eyes to bless Your people
Israel (and all peoples) at every time and every hour with Your peace.
Praised are You, Adonai, who blesses God's people Israel with peace.

46

PRAYER DICTIONARY

שָׁלוֹם
peace

רַב
great

יִשְׂרָאֵל
Israel

עַמְּךָ
your people

וְטוֹב
and may it be good

בְּעֵינֶיךָ
in your eyes

לְבָרֵךְ
to bless

בִּשְׁלוֹמֶךָ
with your peace

PHRASE MATCH

Write the number of the Hebrew phrase next to the correct English meaning.

_____ and may it be good in your eyes

_____ great peace

_____ to bless your people Israel

_____ Israel your people

1. שָׁלוֹם רָב

2. יִשְׂרָאֵל עַמְּךָ

3. וְטוֹב בְּעֵינֶיךָ

4. לְבָרֵךְ אֶת עַמְּךָ יִשְׂרָאֵל

אָבוֹת

גְּבוּרוֹת

קְדוּשָׁה

קְדוּשַׁת הַיּוֹם

עֲבוֹדָה

הוֹדָאָה

▶ בִּרְכַּת שָׁלוֹם

A duck gently gliding in a pond can help make us feel peaceful and calm.

PICK-OUT-PEACE

Look at the שָׁלוֹם רָב prayer on page 46. Circle all the words having to do with "peace."

How many words did you circle?

_____

PRAYER VARIATIONS

Some congregations add the phrase וְאֶת־כָּל־הָעַמִּים ("and all peoples") when they ask God to bless the people of Israel with peace. Whether or not we add this phrase, we all recognize that the prayer asks for peace not just for the people of Israel, but for all the people of the world.

Prayer Building Blocks

שָׁלוֹם רָב עַל־יִשְׂרָאֵל "great peace upon Israel"

שָׁלוֹם רָב means "great peace."

In Hebrew, the word שָׁלוֹם means more than just "peace."

The root שׁלם tells us that "peace," "harmony," "completeness," or "wholeness" is part of a word's meaning.

What do you think the connection is between the different meanings of שָׁלוֹם: "peace," "harmony," "completeness," "wholeness," and even "hello" and "good-bye"?

_____

_____

בִּשְׁלוֹמֶךָ means "with your peace."

Circle the root letters in the word בִּשְׁלוֹמֶךָ.

READING PRACTICE

רָב means "great."

Circle the Hebrew word having to do with "great" in each sentence below.
(Hint: Sometimes the word may have extra letters added.)

Read the sentences aloud.

1. מָה רַבּוּ מַעֲשֶׂיךָ, יְיָ.

2. אַהֲבָה רַבָּה אֲהַבְתָּנוּ, יְיָ אֱלֹהֵינוּ.

3. מְכַלְכֵּל חַיִּים בְּחֶסֶד, מְחַיֶּה הַכֹּל בְּרַחֲמִים רַבִּים.

4. מֹשֶׁה וּבְנֵי יִשְׂרָאֵל לְךָ עָנוּ שִׁירָה בְּשִׂמְחָה רַבָּה.

עַל־יִשְׂרָאֵל עַמְּךָ "upon Israel your people"

יִשְׂרָאֵל means _____ .

עַמְּךָ means "your people" or "your nation."

עַם means _____ .

ךָ is an ending that means _____ .

Look back at the שָׁלוֹם רָב prayer on page 46. Put a star above every word that means "people" or "nation." How many stars did you draw? _____

וְטוֹב בְּעֵינֶיךָ לְבָרֵךְ אֶת־עַמְּךָ יִשְׂרָאֵל

"and may it be good in your eyes to bless your people Israel"

וְטוֹב means "and may it be good."

בְּעֵינֶיךָ means "in your eyes."

עֵינַיִם means "eyes."

בְּ is a prefix meaning _____ .

ךָ is a suffix meaning _____ .

Why do we hope it will be good in God's eyes to bless Israel with peace?

לְבָרֵךְ means "to bless."

Write the root of לְבָרֵךְ. _____ _____ _____

Look back at the שָׁלוֹם רָב prayer. Find another word built on the Hebrew root meaning "bless" and write it here. _____

49

שִׂים שָׁלוֹם

The evening and morning versions of Birkat Shalom are two different ways that the Jews ask God for peace. In Shalom Rav we ask God for general peace in the world; in שִׂים שָׁלוֹם we ask God to inspire us to make peace and to act kindly toward others.

Practice reading שִׂים שָׁלוֹם aloud.

1. שִׂים שָׁלוֹם (בָּעוֹלָם), טוֹבָה וּבְרָכָה, חֵן וָחֶסֶד וְרַחֲמִים

2. עָלֵינוּ וְעַל־כָּל־יִשְׂרָאֵל עַמֶּךָ.

3. בָּרְכֵנוּ, אָבִינוּ, כֻּלָּנוּ כְּאֶחָד, בְּאוֹר פָּנֶיךָ, כִּי בְאוֹר פָּנֶיךָ נָתַתָּ לָּנוּ,

4. יְיָ אֱלֹהֵינוּ, תּוֹרַת חַיִּים, וְאַהֲבַת חֶסֶד, וּצְדָקָה וּבְרָכָה

5. וְרַחֲמִים, וְחַיִּים וְשָׁלוֹם.

6. וְטוֹב בְּעֵינֶיךָ לְבָרֵךְ אֶת־עַמְּךָ יִשְׂרָאֵל (וְאֶת־כָּל־הָעַמִּים)

7. בְּכָל־עֵת וּבְכָל־שָׁעָה בִּשְׁלוֹמֶךָ.

8. בָּרוּךְ אַתָּה, יְיָ, הַמְבָרֵךְ אֶת־עַמּוֹ יִשְׂרָאֵל בַּשָּׁלוֹם.

Grant peace (in the world), goodness and blessing, graciousness and kindness and mercy
(compassion) upon us and upon all Israel Your people.
Bless us, our Parent, all of us as one, with the light of Your face, for with the light of Your face, Adonai
our God, You gave us the Torah of life, and a love of kindness, and righteousness and blessing
and mercy (compassion), and life and peace.
And may it be good in Your eyes to bless Your people Israel (and all peoples)
at every time and at every hour with Your peace.
Praised are You, Adonai, who blesses God's people Israel with peace.

שִׂים

grant, put

טוֹבָה

goodness

חֵן

graciousness

אָבִינוּ

our parent

כֻּלָּנוּ כְּאֶחָד

all of us as one

נָתַתָּ

you gave

תּוֹרַת חַיִּים

Torah of life

וְאַהֲבַת חֶסֶד

and a love of kindness

WORD MATCH

Connect each Hebrew word to its English meaning.

goodness	שִׂים
you gave	טוֹבָה
graciousness	אָבִינוּ
our parent	נָתַתָּ
grant, put	חֵן

Peace comes from within us. A quiet moment during the prayer service can help inspire us to make peace and to act kindly toward others.

PRAYER VARIATIONS

Just as some congregations add the phrase וְאֶת־כָּל־הָעַמִּים ("and all peoples") to the prayer for peace, so do others add the word בָּעוֹלָם ("in the world") to indicate that our wish is for peace for *everyone*.

Prayer Building Blocks

שִׂים שָׁלוֹם "grant peace"

שִׂים usually means "put," but in this prayer we translate it as "grant."

What are we asking God to grant us? _____

The root of שִׂים is שׂימ.

The root שׂימ tells us that "put" is part of a word's meaning.

Read the first sentence of שָׁלוֹם רָב—the evening prayer for peace—and circle the word with the root שׂימ.

שָׁלוֹם רָב עַל־יִשְׂרָאֵל עַמְּךָ תָּשִׂים לְעוֹלָם, כִּי אַתָּה
הוּא מֶלֶךְ אָדוֹן, לְכָל הַשָּׁלוֹם.

Look back at the שִׂים שָׁלוֹם prayer on page 50 and circle all the words having to do with peace. How many words did you circle? _____

ASKING FAVORS

שִׂים שָׁלוֹם asks God to bless us with six favors or gifts. Below are the English meanings of the six gifts we ask of God. Write each one in the blank space next to its matching Hebrew word.

blessing   kindness   peace   mercy   goodness   graciousness

_____ 4. חֵן   _____ 1. שָׁלוֹם

_____ 5. חֶסֶד   _____ 2. טוֹבָה

_____ 6. רַחֲמִים   _____ 3. בְּרָכָה

Which of the six gifts do you consider to be the most important? Why?

_____

_____

בָּרְכֵנוּ, אָבִינוּ, כֻּלָּנוּ כְּאֶחָד   "bless us, our parent, all of us as one"

Write the root of בָּרְכֵנוּ. _____ _____ _____

What does this root mean? _____

What does the ending נוּ mean? _____

אָבִינוּ   literally means "our father."

אָב   means "father."

נוּ   is an ending meaning _____ .

Because God is neither male nor female—not father nor mother—we translate אָבִינוּ as "our parent."

In each sentence below, circle the word that means "our parent." Practice reading the sentences aloud.

1. אָבִינוּ מַלְכֵּנוּ, חָנֵּנוּ וַעֲנֵנוּ, כִּי אֵין בָּנוּ מַעֲשִׂים.

2. אָבִינוּ הָאָב הָרַחֲמָן, הַמְרַחֵם, רַחֵם עָלֵינוּ.

3. סְלַח לָנוּ אָבִינוּ כִּי חָטָאנוּ.

כֻּלָּנוּ כְּאֶחָד   means "all of us as one."

כֻּלָּנוּ   has two parts: כָּל ("all") and the ending נוּ ("us").

כְּאֶחָד   means "as one."

כְּ   means "as."

אֶחָד   means _____ .

Circle אֶחָד in the prayer below.

שְׁמַע יִשְׂרָאֵל יְיָ אֱלֹהֵינוּ יְיָ אֶחָד.

What is the name of this prayer? _____

Explain the meaning of the prayer in your own words.

_____

_____

53

An Ethical Echo

Read these words from Psalm 34:15 in Hebrew and in English.

סוּר מֵרָע וַעֲשֵׂה־טוֹב בַּקֵּשׁ שָׁלוֹם וְרָדְפֵהוּ.

Turn aside from the bad and do good; seek peace and pursue it.

Jewish tradition teaches us that רוֹדֵף שָׁלוֹם—seeking peace—is a holy act. The mitzvah of רוֹדֵף שָׁלוֹם is the act of pursuing peace in our homes, in our communities, and in the world.

The two prayers you are studying in this chapter ask for peace. So do many other prayers, including בִּרְכַּת הַמָּזוֹן—Grace After Meals—where we ask that God "cause peace to dwell among us."

Think About This!

Why do you think we need prayers to help us achieve peace in our homes, in our communities, and in the world?

MAKE PEACE

An ancient rabbi said: "Those who make peace in their homes are as if they made peace in all Israel."

List 4 things you can do to help make your home a more peaceful and loving place.

1. _____

   _____

2. _____

   _____

3. _____

   _____

4. _____

   _____

נָתַתָּ לָנוּ **"you gave to us"**

נָתַתָּ means "you gave."

לָנוּ means "to us."

Break up לָנוּ into its two parts: to _____ לָ

us _____ נוּ

The root of נָתַתָּ is נתן.

(Remember: Sometimes a root letter is missing from a word.)

The root נתן tells us that "give" is part of a word's meaning.

TORAH BLESSINGS

Read the blessings we say when we are called up to read from the Torah.

Underline the words with the root נתן.

BLESSING BEFORE THE TORAH READING:

1. בָּרְכוּ אֶת־יְיָ הַמְבֹרָךְ.

2. בָּרוּךְ יְיָ הַמְבֹרָךְ לְעוֹלָם וָעֶד.

3. בָּרוּךְ אַתָּה, יְיָ אֱלֹהֵינוּ, מֶלֶךְ הָעוֹלָם, אֲשֶׁר בָּחַר־בָּנוּ

4. מִכָּל־הָעַמִּים וְנָתַן־לָנוּ אֶת־תּוֹרָתוֹ.

5. בָּרוּךְ אַתָּה, יְיָ, נוֹתֵן הַתּוֹרָה.

BLESSING AFTER THE TORAH READING:

1. בָּרוּךְ אַתָּה, יְיָ אֱלֹהֵינוּ, מֶלֶךְ הָעוֹלָם, אֲשֶׁר נָתַן לָנוּ

2. תּוֹרַת אֱמֶת וְחַיֵּי עוֹלָם נָטַע בְּתוֹכֵנוּ.

3. בָּרוּךְ אַתָּה, יְיָ, נוֹתֵן הַתּוֹרָה.

How many words did you underline? _____

What did God give us? _____

55

תּוֹרַת חַיִּים, וְאַהֲבַת חֶסֶד "the Torah of life, and a love of kindness"

תּוֹרַת means "the Torah of."

Write the Hebrew word for "Torah." ___תורה___

תּוֹרַת חַיִּים means "the Torah of life."

Write the Hebrew word for "life." ___חיים___

"The Torah of life" could mean: "the law of life," "the Torah telling the story of life," or "the Torah makes life better." Which explanation do you like best and why?

_____

_____

וְאַהֲבַת חֶסֶד means "and a love of kindness."

וְאַהֲבַת means "and a love of."

וְ is a prefix meaning ___and___.

Write the root of אַהֲבַת. ____ ____ ____

What does this root mean? _____

READING PRACTICE

חֶסֶד means "kindness."

Circle חֶסֶד (or its variation) in each line below. Practice reading the phrases aloud.

1. גוֹמֵל חֲסָדִים טוֹבִים וְקוֹנֵה הַכֹּל
2. מְכַלְכֵּל חַיִּים בְּחֶסֶד
3. שִׂים שָׁלוֹם, טוֹבָה וּבְרָכָה, חֵן וָחֶסֶד וְרַחֲמִים
4. הוּא נוֹתֵן לֶחֶם לְכָל־בָּשָׂר כִּי לְעוֹלָם חַסְדּוֹ

Now reread the sentence below from שִׂים שָׁלוֹם describing all the things God has given us. Circle the word meaning "kindness."

תּוֹרַת חַיִּים, וְאַהֲבַת חֶסֶד, וּצְדָקָה וּבְרָכָה וְרַחֲמִים, וְחַיִּים וְשָׁלוֹם.

56

FLUENT READING

After the עֲמִידָה there follows a personal prayer, which is often recited silently. In it we ask for God's help in following the commandments and in choosing our words carefully.

Practice reading the lines below. You will study the last two lines in depth in the next chapter.

1. אֱלֹהַי, נְצֹר לְשׁוֹנִי מֵרָע, וּשְׂפָתַי מִדַּבֵּר מִרְמָה, וְלִמְקַלְלַי

2. נַפְשִׁי תִדּוֹם, וְנַפְשִׁי כֶּעָפָר לַכֹּל תִּהְיֶה. פְּתַח לִבִּי בְּתוֹרָתֶךָ,

3. וּבְמִצְוֹתֶיךָ תִּרְדּוֹף נַפְשִׁי . . .

4. יִהְיוּ לְרָצוֹן אִמְרֵי־פִי וְהֶגְיוֹן לִבִּי לְפָנֶיךָ, יְיָ, צוּרִי וְגוֹאֲלִי.

5. עֹשֶׂה שָׁלוֹם בִּמְרוֹמָיו, הוּא יַעֲשֶׂה שָׁלוֹם עָלֵינוּ וְעַל כָּל-

6. יִשְׂרָאֵל, וְאִמְרוּ אָמֵן.

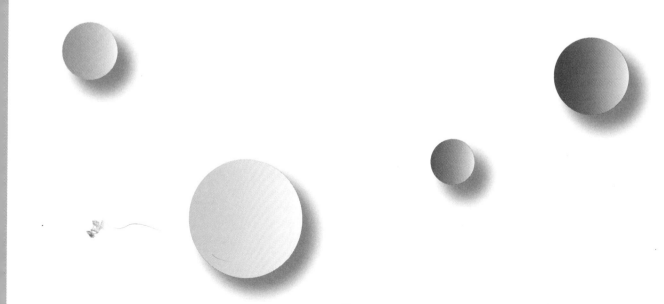

עֲשֵׂה שָׁלוֹם

There are so many kinds of peace that we want—peace between countries (so there is no war), peace between family members (so we don't fight with our little brothers all the time), and peace between friends (so we can continue to play and learn with our classmates and neighbors). There's even something called peace of mind, so we can be happy about who we are and not worry all the time. For all of these reasons, Jews pray for peace.

The עֲשֵׂה שָׁלוֹם ("make peace") prayer is said immediately after the Amidah and asks God to make peace in our lives and in our world.

The Hebrew word for peace is *shalom*; it is also the word for "hello" and "good-bye." You can see how important peace is to the Jews, because we use *shalom* to greet each other and to wish each other well when we part.

Practice reading עֲשֵׂה שָׁלוֹם **aloud.**

1. עֲשֵׂה שָׁלוֹם בִּמְרוֹמָיו, הוּא יַעֲשֶׂה שָׁלוֹם עָלֵינוּ,
2. וְעַל כָּל־יִשְׂרָאֵל. וְאִמְרוּ אָמֵן.

May God who makes peace in the heavens, make peace for us and for all Israel. And say, Amen.

עֹשֶׂה
makes

שָׁלוֹם
peace

יַעֲשֶׂה
(will) make

עָלֵינוּ
for us, on us

וְעַל
and for, and on

כָּל
all

יִשְׂרָאֵל
Israel

וְאִמְרוּ
and say

אָמֵן
Amen

NOTE THE NUMBER

In the circle above each Hebrew word write the number of the correct English meaning.

○	○	○
אָמֵן	יַעֲשֶׂה	שָׁלוֹם
○	○	○
כָּל	וְאִמְרוּ	עָלֵינוּ
○	○	○
יִשְׂרָאֵל	עֹשֶׂה	וְעַל

1. makes   2. and for   3. peace
4. Amen   5. Israel   6. (will) make
7. for us   8. all   9. and say

Many Jews come to the Western Wall to pray for peace for Israel and for all nations.

FAMILY WORDS

There are two sets of family (related) words in the list below.

They are:

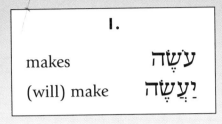

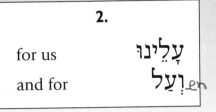

1.	
makes	עֹשֶׂה
(will) make	יַעֲשֶׂה

2.	
for us	עָלֵינוּ
and for	וְעַל

Draw a line between the family words.

עָלֵינוּ   עֹשֶׂה

יַעֲשֶׂה   וְעַל

ROOTS

1. The root of עֹשֶׂה and יַעֲשֶׂה is עשה. עשה means "make."

   Circle the root letters in each word below.

   לְמַעֲשֵׂה   עֹשֶׂה   יַעֲשֶׂה   שֶׁעָשָׂה

   Write the root. ___ ה ___ ש ___ ע ___

   This root means ___ make ___.

2. The root of עָלֵינוּ and וְעַל is עלה. עלה means "go up."

   (Remember: Sometimes a root letter doesn't appear in a Hebrew word.)

   Circle the root letters in these words:

   וַיִּתְעַלֶּה   עֲלִיָּה   עֶלְיוֹן

   Write the root. ___ ה ___ ל ___ ע ___

   This root means ___ go up ___.

   Which of the words above is the honor of being called up to the Torah? _____

PLEASED TO MEET YOU!

In Hebrew we greet each other with the word שָׁלוֹם.

שָׁלוֹם means "hello," "goodbye," and "peace."

(שָׁלוֹם, we know, comes from the Hebrew word שָׁלֵם, which means "complete" or "perfect.")

You have learned the Hebrew word for "name": שֵׁם.

יִ at the end of a word means "my."

If you want to introduce yourself in Hebrew, you say:

שָׁלוֹם, שְׁמִי _____ .

Hello, my name is _____ .

Fill in your Hebrew and your English names on the lines above.

Now introduce yourself to a classmate!

DID YOU KNOW?

According to legend, Jerusalem—יְרוּשָׁלַיִם—the capital city of Israel, is named for peace.

Circle the root letters that mean "peace" in the word below:

King David, who lived 3,000 years ago, was not allowed the honor of building the Holy Temple in יְרוּשָׁלַיִם because he was a man of war. Instead, it was his son, שְׁלֹמֹה, Solomon, who had the honor of building the Holy Temple because he brought peace and prosperity to Israel.

Circle the root letters that mean "peace" in King Solomon's name:

Prayer Building Blocks

עָלֵינוּ "for us"

עָלֵינוּ we know means "for us."

נוּ at the end of a word means _____ .

We ask God to make peace for _____ .

And for who else?

וְעַל כָּל יִשְׂרָאֵל means "and for all _____ ."

וְאִמְרוּ "and say"

וְאִמְרוּ means "and say."

וְ means _____ .

אִמְרוּ means _____ .

The root letters of וְאִמְרוּ are אמר.

אמר tells us that "say" is part of a word's meaning.

READING PRACTICE

Read the following sentences aloud. Circle the words with the root אמר.

1. וְאַל יֹאבַד יִשְׂרָאֵל, הָאוֹמְרִים "שְׁמַע יִשְׂרָאֵל".

2. וַיְהִי בִּנְסֹעַ הָאָרֹן וַיֹּאמֶר מֹשֶׁה.

3. בָּרוּךְ שֶׁאָמַר וְהָיָה הָעוֹלָם, בָּרוּךְ הוּא.

4. בָּרוּךְ אוֹמֵר וְעוֹשֶׂה.

5. וּבְדִבְרֵי קָדְשְׁךָ כָּתוּב לֵאמֹר.

FROM THE TANACH

The quest for peace—for שָׁלוֹם—has always been important to the Jewish people.
Read the following verse from the prophet Isaiah.

And they shall beat their swords into plowshares
And their spears into pruning-hooks;
Nation shall not lift up sword against nation,
Neither shall they learn war any more.

(Isaiah 2:4)

Now read the last two lines of the verse in Hebrew.

לֹא־יִשָּׂא גוֹי אֶל־גּוֹי חֶרֶב
וְלֹא־יִלְמְדוּ עוֹד מִלְחָמָה:

1. Isaiah lived more than 2,500 years ago. Why are his words still important today?

   _____

   _____

2. List the words in the verse that are the opposite of peace.

   _____

   _____

3. In one sentence, describe Isaiah's ideal world.

   _____

   _____

The prophet Micah, who lived at around the same time as Isaiah, spoke almost
the exact words in *his* wish for peace. Why do you think it is significant that the
two prophets spoke almost the identical words?

   _____

A CLOSER LOOK

עֲשֶׂה שָׁלוֹם may be said after the conclusion of the עֲמִידָה. It also appears as part of two other prayers, Grace After Meals (בִּרְכַּת הַמָּזוֹן) and the Kaddish (קַדִּישׁ). When we say עֲשֶׂה שָׁלוֹם at the end of the Kaddish and the Amidah, it is traditional to take three steps backward and to bow to the left and to the right. It is as if the person who is praying is leaving God's presence.

Here is a section of בִּרְכַּת הַמָּזוֹן. Find and underline the עֲשֶׂה שָׁלוֹם prayer.

1. הָרַחֲמָן, הוּא יְזַכֵּנוּ לִימוֹת הַמָּשִׁיחַ, וּלְחַיֵּי הָעוֹלָם הַבָּא:

2. מִגְדּוֹל יְשׁוּעוֹת מַלְכּוֹ, וְעֹשֶׂה־חֶסֶד לִמְשִׁיחוֹ,

3. לְדָוִד וּלְזַרְעוֹ עַד־עוֹלָם. עֹשֶׂה שָׁלוֹם בִּמְרוֹמָיו,

4. הוּא יַעֲשֶׂה שָׁלוֹם עָלֵינוּ וְעַל־כָּל־יִשְׂרָאֵל. וְאִמְרוּ אָמֵן:

Now read this section of the קַדִּישׁ. Find and underline the עֲשֶׂה שָׁלוֹם prayer.

1. יְהֵא שְׁלָמָא רַבָּא מִן שְׁמַיָּא

2. וְחַיִּים עָלֵינוּ וְעַל־כָּל־יִשְׂרָאֵל, וְאִמְרוּ אָמֵן.

3. עֹשֶׂה שָׁלוֹם בִּמְרוֹמָיו, הוּא יַעֲשֶׂה שָׁלוֹם

4. עָלֵינוּ וְעַל־כָּל־יִשְׂרָאֵל, וְאִמְרוּ אָמֵן.

64

An Ethical Echo

There are many ways that we can learn to keep peace within our homes—this peace is called שָׁלוֹם בַּיִת. We can talk things over when we are calm. We can take "time-outs" away from each other when we are angry so that our feelings don't make us lose control. And we can apologize and hug each other to show that respecting one another is more important than proving we are right. Working for peace outside the family must start in the same way—by understanding that people often have different points of view. Respecting each other and thinking about solutions is a better way than fighting to settle differences.

Think About This!

How can you contribute to peace within your family? Perhaps you can try to be more patient with your brothers and sisters, or listen more carefully to what they say. What kinds of things do you and your family members argue over? How do you achieve peace?

Who in your life do you trust?

FLUENT READING

Each line below contains the Hebrew word for "peace."

Practice reading the lines. Then circle the Hebrew word for "peace" in each line.

1. הַפּוֹרֵשׁ סֻכַּת שָׁלוֹם עָלֵינוּ, וְעַל כָּל עַמּוֹ יִשְׂרָאֵל,

וְעַל יְרוּשָׁלָיִם.

2. שָׁלוֹם רָב עַל יִשְׂרָאֵל עַמְּךָ תָּשִׂים לְעוֹלָם.

3. כִּי אַתָּה הוּא מֶלֶךְ אָדוֹן, לְכָל הַשָּׁלוֹם.

4. בָּרוּךְ אַתָּה יְיָ, הַמְבָרֵךְ אֶת עַמּוֹ יִשְׂרָאֵל בַּשָּׁלוֹם.

5. וְרַחֲמִים וְחַיִּים וְשָׁלוֹם, וְכָל־טוֹב, וּמִכָּל־טוֹב לְעוֹלָם אַל־יְחַסְּרֵנוּ.

6. שָׁלוֹם עֲלֵיכֶם, מַלְאֲכֵי הַשָּׁרֵת, מַלְאֲכֵי עֶלְיוֹן.

7. שִׂים שָׁלוֹם, טוֹבָה וּבְרָכָה, חֵן וָחֶסֶד וְרַחֲמִים עָלֵינוּ

וְעַל כָּל יִשְׂרָאֵל עַמֶּךָ.

8. בָּרוּךְ אַתָּה, יְיָ אֱלֹהֵינוּ, מֶלֶךְ הָעוֹלָם, יוֹצֵר אוֹר

וּבוֹרֵא חֹשֶׁךְ עֹשֶׂה שָׁלוֹם וּבוֹרֵא אֶת הַכֹּל.

FRIDAY NIGHT SERVICE

Are there special occasions you just can't wait for—that you look forward to for weeks in advance? Maybe it's your school's big holiday concert. Or maybe it's summer vacation, when you're off to camp with lots of other kids to swim, play softball, and tell ghost stories.

Shabbat is that kind of occasion for many Jews, who look forward to it all week long. Shabbat is a peaceful end to our week—a day to devote to ourselves, our family, and friends. It's a day when we can put aside the weekly demands of school and work and enjoy an unhurried pace. Rabbi Abraham Joshua Heschel called Shabbat "a palace in time"—a holy place that opens its doors to us once a week, inviting us to enter.

Friday night—the beginning of Shabbat—is an important time to spend with our families. Often the table is set for a special celebration—perhaps with a fancy tablecloth and, of course, candles, wine, and hallah. We say the blessings, perhaps sing Shabbat songs, and eat a special meal.

The Friday night Kabbalat Shabbat service marks the beginning of Shabbat in the synagogue. The prayers of the service speak of God the Creator, of the promises God made to the Jews, and of the wondrous gift of Shabbat. We pray as a community with our friends, our neighbors, and our family. And we say "hi" to them as well, catching up with what has happened since last Shabbat, and talking about what to expect in the week to come.

לְכָה דוֹדִי

How do you welcome people you love? Maybe you give your grandmother a kiss and your favorite cousin a hug. Or maybe you and your friends exchange "high fives." These greetings are signs that you are happy to see them. On Friday nights, we welcome Shabbat with greetings that express our joy at its arrival—a service called Kabbalat Shabbat ("Welcoming Shabbat" or "Receiving Shabbat") and a hymn called לְכָה דוֹדִי.

In Lechah Dodi, we greet Shabbat as if it were a bride or a queen—radiant and beautiful. We have anticipated the arrival of Shabbat all week, just as we look forward to the arrival of those we love the most.

Practice reading the first verses of לְכָה דוֹדִי **and the last verse aloud.**

1. לְכָה דוֹדִי לִקְרַאת כַּלָּה, פְּנֵי שַׁבָּת נְקַבְּלָה:

2. שָׁמוֹר וְזָכוֹר בְּדִבּוּר אֶחָד הִשְׁמִיעָנוּ אֵל הַמְיֻחָד

3. יְיָ אֶחָד וּשְׁמוֹ אֶחָד לְשֵׁם וּלְתִפְאֶרֶת וְלִתְהִלָּה:

4. לִקְרַאת שַׁבָּת לְכוּ וְנֵלְכָה כִּי הִיא מְקוֹר הַבְּרָכָה

5. מֵרֹאשׁ מִקֶּדֶם נְסוּכָה סוֹף מַעֲשֶׂה בְּמַחֲשָׁבָה תְּחִלָּה:

6. בּוֹאִי בְשָׁלוֹם עֲטֶרֶת בַּעְלָהּ גַּם בְּשִׂמְחָה וּבְצָהֳלָה,

7. תּוֹךְ אֱמוּנֵי עַם סְגֻלָּה, בֹּאִי כַלָּה, בֹּאִי כַלָּה:

Let us go, my beloved, to meet (toward) the Bride, let us greet Shabbat.
"Keep" and "Remember" in one Commandment, the one and the only God made us hear.
Adonai is One and God's name is One, for honor and glory and praise.
To greet (toward) Shabbat come let us go, for it is the source of blessing.
From the beginning of time Shabbat is appointed; though last in creation, it was first in God's thought.
Come in peace, crown of your husband, in joy and in gladness,
In the midst of the faithful of the treasured people. Come, O Bride! Come, O Bride!

PRAYER DICTIONARY

לְכָה
go

דּוֹדִי
my beloved

כַּלָּה
bride

פְּנֵי
the face of

נְקַבְּלָה
let us receive

שָׁמוֹר
keep

זָכוֹר
remember

בֹּאִי
come

WORD MATCH

Connect the word to its English meaning.

keep   לְכָה

come   שָׁמוֹר

go   זָכוֹר

remember   בֹּאִי

In Lechah Dodi, we compare Shabbat to a bride. How do you feel when you see a bride?

WHAT'S MISSING?

Fill in the Hebrew word that completes each phrase.

1. לְכָה _____ לִקְרַאת כַּלָּה
   my beloved

2. _____ שַׁבָּת נְקַבְּלָה
   the face of

3. _____ וְזָכוֹר בְּדִבּוּר אֶחָד
   keep

4. בֹּאִי _____
   bride

69

PRAYER BACKGROUND

The custom of greeting Shabbat is an ancient one. The rabbis of the Talmud put on their robes and went out to welcome Shabbat at sunset on Friday evenings. Jewish mystics in the sixteenth century welcomed Shabbat with the words, "Come, let us go to greet the Shabbat Queen." They would go out into the fields on a Friday evening singing songs to welcome Shabbat.

Today, we do not go into the fields, but we do continue to sing the most famous of those songs to welcome Shabbat: לְכָה דוֹדִי.

לְכָה דוֹדִי was written by Rabbi Shlomo Halevi Alkabetz about 500 years ago, which makes this prayer relatively new. The שְׁמַע, for example, became part of our prayer service nearly 2,000 years ago!

It was the custom of the ancient rabbis to go out into the fields at sunset on Friday to welcome Shabbat.

A POETIC DEVICE

לְכָה דוֹדִי is an acrostic. In an acrostic, the first letters of certain words spell out a new "secret" word or form the *alef bet*.

You will find the complete לְכָה דוֹדִי on page 75.

Circle the first letter of lines 2, 4, 6, 8, 10, 12, 14, 16.

Write the 8 letters you have circled in the spaces below.

Can you figure out whose name you have written?

____ ____ ____ ____ ____ ____ ____ ____

Prayer Building Blocks

לְכָה דוֹדִי "let us go, my beloved"

לְכָה means "let us go."

The root of לְכָה is הלכ.

The root הלכ tell us that "go" or "walk" is part of a word's meaning.

דוֹדִי means "my beloved."

"My beloved" may refer to God, who we ask to come with us to greet Shabbat, or it may refer to the other worshipers in the synagogue.

לִקְרַאת כַּלָּה "to meet (toward) the bride"

The central metaphor of לְכָה דוֹדִי is the description of Shabbat as a bride.

כַּלָּה means "bride."

The Hebrew word for *groom* is חָתָן.

Complete the phrase.

groom and bride   _____ וְ חָתָן

Read this בְּרָכָה from the wedding ceremony.

בָּרוּךְ אַתָּה יְיָ, מְשַׂמֵּחַ חָתָן עִם הַכַּלָּה.

Praised are You, Adonai, who brings joy to the groom and the bride.

Circle the word for "groom."

Underline the word for "the bride."

פָּנִים   means "face."

פְּנֵי   literally means "the face of."

לְקַבֵּל   means "to greet" or "to receive."

נְקַבְּלָה   means "let us greet" or "let us receive."

The Hebrew expression לְקַבֵּל אֶת פְּנֵי... literally means "to receive the face of . . . ." However, we translate the expression as "to welcome" or "to greet." The poet is asking God, the "beloved," to come with us to welcome or to greet Shabbat.

ROOTS

The root letters of נְקַבְּלָה are קבל.

The root קבל tells us that "receive" or "welcome" is part of a word's meaning.

The service in which we welcome Shabbat on a Friday night is called קַבָּלַת שַׁבָּת, Kabbalat Shabbat. Upon conclusion of this brief service, the evening service (מַעֲרִיב) begins.

Circle the root letters of the word קַבָּלַת.

What does this root mean?

_____

We begin the Shabbat celebration by lighting candles on a Friday evening.

72

שָׁמוֹר וְזָכוֹר "keep and remember"

שָׁמוֹר means "keep."

The root letters of שָׁמוֹר are שמר.

The root שמר tells us that "keep" or "guard" are part of the word's meaning.

(Perhaps you have heard the expression שׁוֹמֵר שַׁבָּת—
one who keeps or observes Shabbat.)

- -

זָכוֹר means "remember."

The root letters of זָכוֹר are זכר.

The root זכר tells us that "remember" is part of the word's meaning.

READING PRACTICE

Read the phrases below. Circle the word with the root שמר in each line.

1. וְשָׁמְרוּ בְּנֵי יִשְׂרָאֵל אֶת הַשַּׁבָּת

2. שָׁמוֹר אֶת יוֹם הַשַּׁבָּת לְקַדְּשׁוֹ

3. לִשְׁמֹעַ לִלְמֹד וּלְלַמֵּד, לִשְׁמֹר וְלַעֲשׂוֹת

4. יִשְׂמְחוּ בְמַלְכוּתְךָ שׁוֹמְרֵי שַׁבָּת וְקוֹרְאֵי עֹנֶג

5. שׁוֹמֵר יְיָ אֶת כָּל אֹהֲבָיו

DID YOU KNOW?

The Ten Commandments appear twice in the Torah. In the Book of Deuteronomy we are told to שָׁמוֹר— "keep" or "guard"—Shabbat. In the Book of Exodus the commandment tells us to זָכוֹר—"remember"—Shabbat.

We light at least two candles on Shabbat to represent the two commandments to observe Shabbat: זָכוֹר אֶת יוֹם הַשַּׁבָּת and שָׁמוֹר אֶת יוֹם הַשַּׁבָּת.

73

בּוֹאִי בְשָׁלוֹם...בּֽאִי כַלָּה   *"come in peace . . . come, O bride"*

בּוֹאִי is a command word meaning "come."

בְשָׁלוֹם means "in peace."

בְ means _____ .

שָׁלוֹם means _____ .

כַלָּה we know means "bride."

בֹּאִי כַלָּה means _____ .

ROOTS

The root letters of בֹּאִי are בוא.

The root בוא tells us that "come" is part of a word's meaning.

Read the following prayer phrases. Underline the words with the root בוא.

(Note: Sometimes the root letter ו is missing.)

1. בֹּאוּ וְנֵצֵא לִקְרַאת שַׁבָּת הַמַּלְכָּה

2. אֲנִי מַאֲמִין בֶּאֱמוּנָה שְׁלֵמָה בְּבִיאַת הַמָּשִׁיחַ

3. בּוֹאֲכֶם לְשָׁלוֹם, מַלְאֲכֵי הַשָּׁלוֹם

4. וַאֲנִי בְּרֹב חַסְדְּךָ אָבוֹא בֵיתֶךָ

5. יַעֲלֶה וְיָבֹא וְיִזָּכֵר זִכְרוֹנֵנוּ

Think About This!

In many congregations we stand up before singing the final verse of לְכָה דוֹדִי (the verse that begins with the words בּוֹאִי בְשָׁלוֹם). We face the door of the sanctuary in anticipation of the arrival of Shabbat. And, when we say בֹּאִי כַלָּה, בֹּאִי כַלָּה, we bow to the left and right.

How do you picture Shabbat in the scene above? _____

_____

74

Practice reading the complete לְכָה דוֹדִי.

1. לְכָה דוֹדִי לִקְרַאת כַּלָּה פְּנֵי שַׁבָּת נְקַבְּלָה:

2. שָׁמוֹר וְזָכוֹר בְּדִבּוּר אֶחָד הִשְׁמִיעָנוּ אֵל הַמְיֻחָד

3. יְיָ אֶחָד וּשְׁמוֹ אֶחָד לְשֵׁם וּלְתִפְאֶרֶת וְלִתְהִלָּה:

4. לִקְרַאת שַׁבָּת לְכוּ וְנֵלְכָה כִּי הִיא מְקוֹר הַבְּרָכָה

5. מֵרֹאשׁ מִקֶּדֶם נְסוּכָה סוֹף מַעֲשֶׂה בְּמַחֲשָׁבָה תְּחִלָּה:

6. מִקְדַּשׁ מֶלֶךְ עִיר מְלוּכָה קוּמִי צְאִי מִתּוֹךְ הַהֲפֵכָה

7. רַב לָךְ שֶׁבֶת בְּעֵמֶק הַבָּכָא וְהוּא יַחֲמוֹל עָלַיִךְ חֶמְלָה:

8. הִתְנַעֲרִי מֵעָפָר קוּמִי לִבְשִׁי בִּגְדֵי תִפְאַרְתֵּךְ עַמִּי

9. עַל־יַד בֶּן־יִשַׁי בֵּית־הַלַּחְמִי קָרְבָה אֶל נַפְשִׁי גְאָלָהּ:

10. הִתְעוֹרְרִי הִתְעוֹרְרִי כִּי בָא אוֹרֵךְ קוּמִי אוֹרִי

11. עוּרִי עוּרִי שִׁיר דַּבֵּרִי כְּבוֹד יְיָ עָלַיִךְ נִגְלָה:

12. לֹא תֵבוֹשִׁי וְלֹא תִכָּלְמִי מַה־תִּשְׁתּוֹחֲחִי וּמַה־תֶּהֱמִי

13. בָּךְ יֶחֱסוּ עֲנִיֵּי עַמִּי וְנִבְנְתָה עִיר עַל־תִּלָּהּ:

14. וְהָיוּ לִמְשִׁסָּה שֹׁאסָיִךְ וְרָחֲקוּ כָּל־מְבַלְּעָיִךְ

15. יָשִׂישׂ עָלַיִךְ אֱלֹהָיִךְ כִּמְשׂוֹשׂ חָתָן עַל־כַּלָּה:

16. יָמִין וּשְׂמֹאל תִּפְרוֹצִי וְאֶת־יְיָ תַּעֲרִיצִי

17. עַל־יַד אִישׁ בֶּן־פַּרְצִי וְנִשְׂמְחָה וְנָגִילָה:

18. בּוֹאִי בְשָׁלוֹם עֲטֶרֶת בַּעְלָהּ גַּם בְּשִׂמְחָה וּבְצָהֳלָה

19. תּוֹךְ אֱמוּנֵי עַם סְגֻלָּה בֹּאִי כַלָּה, בֹּאִי כַלָּה:

Do you have something precious that you protect or guard? Maybe it's a diary where you write down your secret thoughts and wishes, kept hidden under your pillow. Or maybe you have a bike you received as a birthday present, that you keep safe with a lock during school hours.

In a similar way, the Jewish people consider Shabbat to be sacred, and guard it as a gift from God. וְשָׁמְרוּ ("and [you] shall keep" or "and [you] shall guard") comes from the Torah, and reminds us of our promise to God to guard, cherish, and observe Shabbat and keep it holy. V'shamru is said before the Amidah during the Friday night service. In reciting it, we declare that we are guarding Shabbat because it is God's special creation—and we remember that by celebrating Shabbat we are strengthening our ties to God.

Practice reading וְשָׁמְרוּ aloud.

1. וְשָׁמְרוּ בְנֵי־יִשְׂרָאֵל אֶת־הַשַּׁבָּת, לַעֲשׂוֹת אֶת־הַשַּׁבָּת

2. לְדֹרֹתָם בְּרִית עוֹלָם. בֵּינִי וּבֵין בְּנֵי יִשְׂרָאֵל אוֹת הִיא לְעֹלָם,

3. כִּי שֵׁשֶׁת יָמִים עָשָׂה יְיָ אֶת־הַשָּׁמַיִם וְאֶת־הָאָרֶץ,

4. וּבַיּוֹם הַשְּׁבִיעִי שָׁבַת וַיִּנָּפַשׁ.

And the children of Israel shall keep the Shabbat, to make the Shabbat
as an eternal covenant for their generations. Between Me and the children of Israel it is a sign forever,
that in six days Adonai made the heavens and the earth,
and on the seventh day Adonai rested and was refreshed.

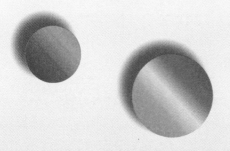

Hebrew	English
וְשָׁמְרוּ	and shall keep
בְּנֵי	the children of
יִשְׂרָאֵל	Israel
לַעֲשׂוֹת	to make
לְדֹרֹתָם	for their generations
בְּרִית	covenant
עוֹלָם	eternal
הַשָּׁמַיִם	the heavens
הָאָרֶץ	the earth
יוֹם הַשְּׁבִיעִי	the seventh day
שָׁבַת	rested

SEARCH AND CIRCLE

Circle the Hebrew word that means the same as the English.

Israel	יְצְחָק	יִשְׂרָאֵל	יְרוּשָׁלַיִם
eternal	עוֹלָם	אַבְרָהָם	אָמֵן
the heavens	הַשָּׁמַיִם	הָעַמִּים	הַמְּלָכִים
covenant	דִּבּוּר	כַּלָּה	בְּרִית
the earth	הַתּוֹרָה	הָאָרֶץ	הַשַּׁבָּת

SHABBAT MATCH

Use the words in the box below to write the English meaning above each Hebrew word.

for their generations	to make	the children of
rested	and shall keep	the seventh day

לְדֹרֹתָם	וְשָׁמְרוּ	יוֹם הַשְּׁבִיעִי

בְּנֵי	שָׁבַת	לַעֲשׂוֹת

Prayer Building Blocks

וְשָׁמְרוּ בְנֵי־יִשְׂרָאֵל אֶת־הַשַּׁבָּת

"and the children of Israel shall keep the Shabbat"

וְשָׁמְרוּ means "and shall keep."

What must the Jews keep? Write your answer in Hebrew. _____

What is the root of וְשָׁמְרוּ? _____ _____ _____

What does this root mean? _____

Circle the word with the same root in this sentence.

שָׁמוֹר וְזָכוֹר בְּדִבּוּר אֶחָד

In which hymn is this line found? _____

Give two examples of what it means to *keep* Shabbat.

1. _____

2. _____

An Ethical Echo

Just as we guard Shabbat, so are there other things that we guard. שְׁמִירַת הַלָּשׁוֹן— "guarding the tongue"—is a mitzvah that commands us not to gossip, spread rumors, or tell lies. When we are careless about what we say, we indulge in לְשׁוֹן הָרַע— "the tongue of evil." Why would this kind of talk be called "the tongue of evil"? Why are we taught to think before we speak? Do you think this is good advice?

Think About This!

There is an old saying that "sticks and stones may break my bones but names can never hurt me." Do you agree with these words? Why? Do you think that there are other ways to hurt someone besides physically?

78

בְּנֵי־יִשְׂרָאֵל "the children of Israel"

בְּנֵי or בְּנֵי means "the children of."

בָּנִים means "children."

בָּנִים is the plural of בֵּן.

בֵּן means _____.

Circle the part of בָּנִים that shows it is plural.   בָּנִים

יִשְׂרָאֵל we know means _____.

בְּנֵי־יִשְׂרָאֵל means _____.

DID YOU KNOW?

Many people have nicknames. Maybe your older sister calls you "Kid," or maybe you have a friend you call "Hotshot" because he's great at basketball. Or perhaps you know an Edwin who likes to be called "Ned." In the same way, one of our ancestors, Jacob, was given a new name—"Israel"—when he wrestled with an angel of God. "Israel" comes from the Hebrew meaning "to struggle with God." And the descendants of Jacob— the Jews—are known as the children of Israel.

It's so easy to start to gossip. Stop and think before you speak.

לַעֲשׂוֹת אֶת־הַשַּׁבָּת לְדֹרֹתָם בְּרִית עוֹלָם

"to make the Shabbat as an eternal covenant for their generations"

לַעֲשׂוֹת means "to make."

The root of לַעֲשׂוֹת is עשׂה.

What is the meaning of this root? _____

Underline the word with the same root in this line from וְשָׁמְרוּ:

כִּי שֵׁשֶׁת יָמִים עָשָׂה יְיָ אֶת־הַשָּׁמַיִם וְאֶת־הָאָרֶץ

Now underline the words with the same root in עֹשֶׂה שָׁלוֹם.

עֹשֶׂה שָׁלוֹם בִּמְרוֹמָיו, הוּא יַעֲשֶׂה שָׁלוֹם עָלֵינוּ
וְעַל כָּל־יִשְׂרָאֵל

בְּרִית עוֹלָם means "eternal covenant."

עוֹלָם can mean "eternal (forever)" or "world."

DID YOU KNOW?

As a bond with God, our ancestor Abraham agreed to circumcise his son, Isaac, in return for God's gift of watching over the Jewish people. To this day, Jewish baby boys are circumcised in a בְּרִית מִילָה ceremony (many people call it a *bris*) when they are eight days old. We now celebrate the birth of a baby girl, too, with a ceremony called שִׂמְחַת בַּת ("joyful celebration for a daughter"). A *bris* or *simhat bat* is the grandest celebration of all—a celebration of the day you were born!

A SPECIAL AGREEMENT

God told the children of Israel to make Shabbat an "eternal covenant" for all their generations.

A covenant—בְּרִית— is an agreement. It implies a special relationship between two parties who then have obligations to each other. In the בְּרִית between God and the Jewish people, the Jews are obligated to fulfill God's mitzvot and, in return, God promises to give the Jews the land of Israel and to watch over them.

Part of the Jews' obligation is to keep Shabbat throughout all generations.

לְדֹרֹתָם means "for (all) their generations."

לְ means "for."

דוֹר means "generation."

דוֹרוֹת is the plural for דוֹר.

Circle the part of דוֹרוֹת that shows it is plural.   דוֹרוֹת

Circle the Hebrew phrase that means "from generation to generation" in the sentence below. Write the name of the prayer from which it comes. _____

(Hint: Look back at page 28 in your textbook.)

לְדוֹר וָדוֹר נַגִּיד גָּדְלֶךָ, וּלְנֵצַח נְצָחִים קְדֻשָּׁתְךָ נַקְדִּישׁ.

ם ָ is a word ending (suffix) that means "their" or "them."

Circle the word ending in each of these words.

וְשִׁנַּנְתָּם   בָּם   וּקְשַׁרְתָּם   וּכְתַבְתָּם   וּבִתְפַלְתָּם

What does this word ending mean? _____

עָשָׂה יְיָ אֶת־הַשָּׁמַיִם וְאֶת־הָאָרֶץ

"Adonai made the heavens and the earth"

אֶת־הַשָּׁמַיִם וְאֶת־הָאָרֶץ means "the heavens and the earth."

הַשָּׁמַיִם means _____ .

שָׁמַיִם means _____ .

הָאָרֶץ means _____ .

אֶרֶץ means _____ .

Circle the phrase for "the heavens and the earth" that is written in the very first line of the Torah.

בְּרֵאשִׁית בָּרָא אֱלֹהִים אֵת הַשָּׁמַיִם וְאֵת הָאָרֶץ:

In the beginning God created the heavens and the earth.

וּבַיּוֹם הַשְּׁבִיעִי שָׁבַת וַיִּנָּפַשׁ

"and on the seventh day Adonai rested and was refreshed"

וּבַיּוֹם הַשְּׁבִיעִי means "and on the seventh day."

וּבַיּוֹם means "and on the day."

וּ means _____ .

בַ means "on the " or "in the."

יוֹם means "day."

יוֹם הַשְּׁבִיעִי is another name for _____ .

REST ON SHABBAT

שָׁבַת means "rested."

Do you see the connection between שָׁבַת—rested—and שַׁבָּת—Shabbat?

Both words have the root שבת.

The root שבת tells us that "rested" or "stopped working" is part of a word's meaning.

Read the words below. Circle the root letters שבת in these words.

שַׁבַּת הַגָּדוֹל   תִּשְׁבֹּת   שַׁבָּתוֹן   וַיִּשְׁבֹּת

What root do the words above share? _____ _____ _____

What does this root mean? _____

The first mention of a day of rest appears in the Creation story: *"And God rested on the seventh day from all the work God had made. And God blessed the seventh day, and made it holy because on it God rested from all the work, which God in creating had made"* (Genesis 2:2–3).

Read the same Torah passage in Hebrew below. Underline the two words that mean "rested."

1. וַיִּשְׁבֹּת בַּיּוֹם הַשְּׁבִיעִי מִכָּל־מְלַאכְתּוֹ אֲשֶׁר עָשָׂה:

2. וַיְבָרֶךְ אֱלֹהִים אֶת־יוֹם הַשְּׁבִיעִי וַיְקַדֵּשׁ אֹתוֹ כִּי בוֹ
שָׁבַת מִכָּל־מְלַאכְתּוֹ אֲשֶׁר־בָּרָא אֱלֹהִים לַעֲשׂוֹת:

Now circle the two words with the root meaning "make" (עשה).

Draw a squiggly line below the word with the root meaning "bless" (ברכ).

Put a star above the word with the root meaning "holy" (קדש).

IN YOUR OWN WORDS

Explain in your own words why we observe Shabbat.

_____

_____

You have learned that we say וְשָׁמְרוּ before the עֲמִידָה on a Friday evening. On Shabbat morning וְשָׁמְרוּ is *part* of the עֲמִידָה. Try to find וְשָׁמְרוּ in *your* prayerbook.

BACK TO THE SOURCES

The prayer וְשָׁמְרוּ comes from the Torah. God said these words to Moses just before giving him the Ten Commandments.

This is a section from the Book of Exodus (31:15–18).

Can you find and read וְשָׁמְרוּ ?

טו שֵׁשֶׁת יָמִים יֵעָשֶׂה מְלָאכָה וּבַיּוֹם
הַשְּׁבִיעִי שַׁבַּת שַׁבָּתוֹן קֹדֶשׁ לַיהוָה כָּל־הָעֹשֶׂה מְלָאכָה

טז בְּיוֹם הַשַּׁבָּת מוֹת יוּמָת: וְשָׁמְרוּ בְנֵי־יִשְׂרָאֵל אֶת־הַשַּׁבָּת

יז לַעֲשׂוֹת אֶת־הַשַּׁבָּת לְדֹרֹתָם בְּרִית עוֹלָם: בֵּינִי וּבֵין
בְּנֵי יִשְׂרָאֵל אוֹת הִוא לְעֹלָם כִּי־שֵׁשֶׁת יָמִים עָשָׂה
יְהוָה אֶת־הַשָּׁמַיִם וְאֶת־הָאָרֶץ וּבַיּוֹם הַשְּׁבִיעִי שָׁבַת

יח וַיִּנָּפַשׁ: וַיִּתֵּן אֶל־מֹשֶׁה כְּכַלֹּתוֹ לְדַבֵּר אִתּוֹ
בְּהַר סִינַי שְׁנֵי לֻחֹת הָעֵדֻת לֻחֹת אֶבֶן כְּתֻבִים בְּאֶצְבַּע
אֱלֹהִים:

Many of our prayers, including the Sh'ma, Mi Chamochah, and V'shamru, come from the Torah itself.

FLUENT READING

Shortly before we sing וְשָׁמְרוּ on a Friday night, we recite אַהֲבַת עוֹלָם. This blessing focuses on God's love for Israel, which God shows by giving us the Torah and mitzvot.

Practice reading אַהֲבַת עוֹלָם.

1. אַהֲבַת עוֹלָם בֵּית יִשְׂרָאֵל עַמְּךָ אָהַבְתָּ: תּוֹרָה וּמִצְוֹת,

2. חֻקִּים וּמִשְׁפָּטִים אוֹתָנוּ לִמַּדְתָּ.

3. עַל־כֵּן, יְיָ אֱלֹהֵינוּ, בְּשָׁכְבֵּנוּ וּבְקוּמֵנוּ נָשִׂיחַ בְּחֻקֶּיךָ,

4. וְנִשְׂמַח בְּדִבְרֵי תוֹרָתֶךָ וּבְמִצְוֹתֶיךָ לְעוֹלָם וָעֶד.

5. כִּי הֵם חַיֵּינוּ וְאֹרֶךְ יָמֵינוּ, וּבָהֶם נֶהְגֶּה יוֹמָם וָלַיְלָה.

6. וְאַהֲבָתְךָ אַל־תָּסִיר מִמֶּנּוּ לְעוֹלָמִים!

7. בָּרוּךְ אַתָּה, יְיָ, אוֹהֵב עַמּוֹ יִשְׂרָאֵל.

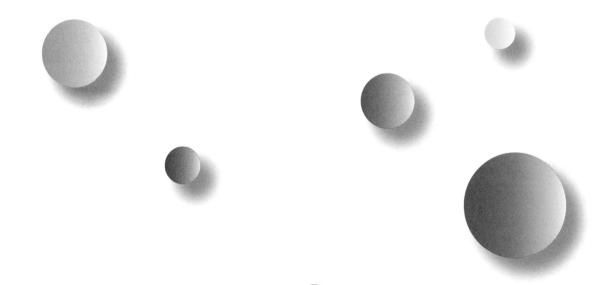

85

שָׁלוֹם עֲלֵיכֶם

Do you and your dad ever turn the radio up full-blast in the car and sing along together? Or maybe you and your friends watch a music video and sing the latest songs as a group. Singing together builds a bond—a feeling of togetherness and community.

We sing the שָׁלוֹם עֲלֵיכֶם hymn at home on Friday night, between lighting the candles and reciting the Kiddush. As we sing it, we strengthen our ties to each other and the good feelings we share.

Shalom Aleichem means "peace be upon you" and is another way we express our hope for peace and well-being.

Practice reading שָׁלוֹם עֲלֵיכֶם aloud.

1. שָׁלוֹם עֲלֵיכֶם, מַלְאֲכֵי הַשָּׁרֵת, מַלְאֲכֵי עֶלְיוֹן,

2. מִמֶּלֶךְ מַלְכֵי הַמְּלָכִים, הַקָּדוֹשׁ בָּרוּךְ הוּא.

3. בּוֹאֲכֶם לְשָׁלוֹם, מַלְאֲכֵי הַשָּׁלוֹם, מַלְאֲכֵי עֶלְיוֹן,

4. מִמֶּלֶךְ מַלְכֵי הַמְּלָכִים, הַקָּדוֹשׁ בָּרוּךְ הוּא.

5. בָּרְכוּנִי לְשָׁלוֹם, מַלְאֲכֵי הַשָּׁלוֹם, מַלְאֲכֵי עֶלְיוֹן,

6. מִמֶּלֶךְ מַלְכֵי הַמְּלָכִים, הַקָּדוֹשׁ בָּרוּךְ הוּא.

7. צֵאתְכֶם לְשָׁלוֹם, מַלְאֲכֵי הַשָּׁלוֹם, מַלְאֲכֵי עֶלְיוֹן,

8. מִמֶּלֶךְ מַלְכֵי הַמְּלָכִים, הַקָּדוֹשׁ בָּרוּךְ הוּא.

Peace upon you, O ministering angels, angels of the Supreme,
From the Ruler of rulers, the Holy Blessed One.

Come in peace, O angels of peace, angels of the Supreme,
From the Ruler of rulers, the Holy Blessed One.

Bless me with peace, O angels of peace, angels of the Supreme,
From the Ruler of rulers, the Holy Blessed One.

Depart in peace, O angels of peace, angels of the Supreme,
From the Ruler of rulers, the Holy Blessed One.

PRAYER DICTIONARY

שָׁלוֹם
peace

עֲלֵיכֶם
upon you

מַלְאֲכֵי
angels of

עֶלְיוֹן
(the) Supreme

מֶלֶךְ מַלְכֵי הַמְּלָכִים
Ruler of rulers

הַקָּדוֹשׁ בָּרוּךְ הוּא
the Holy Blessed One

בּוֹאֲכֶם
come

בָּרְכוּנִי
bless me

צֵאתְכֶם
depart

SERIOUS SYNONYMS

Write the three Hebrew words or phrases from the Prayer Dictionary that are names we use to refer to God. Then write their English meanings.

ENGLISH	HEBREW	
_____	_____	.1
_____	_____	.2
_____	_____	.3

ACTION WORDS

Write the English meaning for each Hebrew word below.

בָּרְכוּנִי	בּוֹאֲכֶם	צֵאתְכֶם
_____	_____	_____

Do you recognize the words on this sign? What do they mean?

THE LEGEND OF THE HYMN

The Shalom Aleichem hymn is based on a legend from the Talmud in which two angels—one good, one evil—escort each Jew home from the synagogue on a Friday evening. If the home is ready for Shabbat with the table set and candles lit, the good angel says: "May it be God's will that it also be so next Shabbat." The evil angel is forced to answer, "Amen." But if nothing is prepared for Shabbat, the evil angel says: "May it be God's will that it also be so next Shabbat," and the good angel has to respond, "Amen." In the song we greet the accompanying angels, bless them, and ask for their blessing in return.

FOLLOW THE PATH HOME

Follow the route from the synagogue to the house by filling in the missing English words.

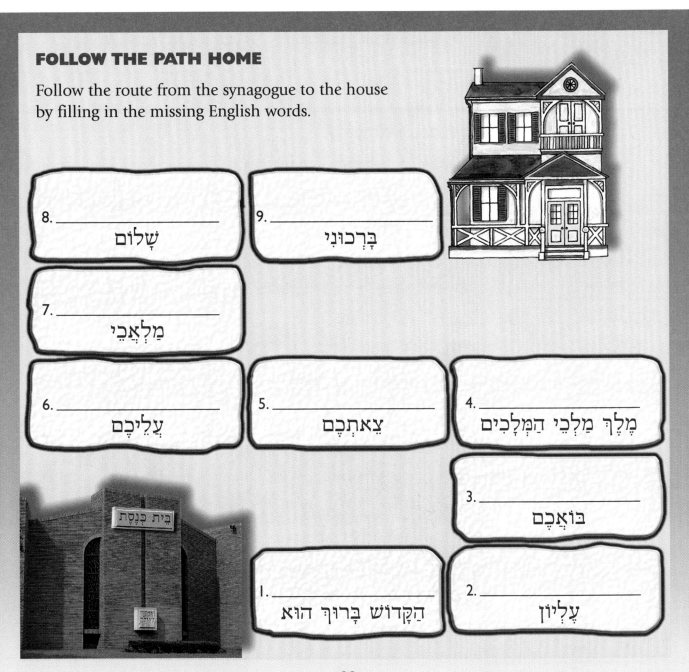

8. _____ שָׁלוֹם

9. _____ בָּרְכוּנִי

7. _____ מַלְאֲכֵי

6. _____ עֲלֵיכֶם

5. _____ צֵאתְכֶם

4. _____ מֶלֶךְ מַלְכֵי הַמְּלָכִים

3. _____ בּוֹאֲכֶם

1. _____ הַקָּדוֹשׁ בָּרוּךְ הוּא

2. _____ עֶלְיוֹן

88

Prayer Building Blocks

שָׁלוֹם עֲלֵיכֶם "peace upon you"

שָׁלוֹם means _____ .

עֲלֵיכֶם means "upon you."

The word ending (suffix) כֶם means "you" (plural).

Circle the part of the following word that means "upon" or "on": עֲלֵיכֶם

Circle the suffix in these words from שָׁלוֹם עֲלֵיכֶם.

צֵאתְכֶם   בּוֹאֲכֶם

You have studied 3 other prayers with the word שָׁלוֹם in their names.

Write the names of the 3 prayers.

(Hint: Look at the Table of Contents in the front of your book.)

1. _____

2. _____

3. _____

4. שָׁלוֹם עֲלֵיכֶם

מַלְאֲכֵי עֶלְיוֹן "angels of the Supreme"

מַלְאֲכֵי means "angels of."

מַלְאָכִים means "angels."

מַלְאָכִים is the plural of מַלְאָךְ.

Circle the part of מַלְאָכִים that shows it is plural. מַלְאָכִים

עֶלְיוֹן means "Supreme."

Who is "Supreme"? _____

What part of the word עֶלְיוֹן do you recognize? Write it here. _____

What does this word part mean? _____

מִמֶּלֶךְ מַלְכֵי הַמְּלָכִים "from the Ruler of rulers"

Who is the Ruler of rulers? _____

Write the root for the words in the phrase מִמֶּלֶךְ מַלְכֵי הַמְּלָכִים.

_____ _____ _____

What does this root mean? _____

The prefix מִ means "from." Circle the prefix in this word: מִמֶּלֶךְ

הַקָּדוֹשׁ בָּרוּךְ הוּא "the Holy Blessed One"

Who is "the Holy Blessed One"? _____

הַקָּדוֹשׁ means "the holy."

הַ means _____.

קָדוֹשׁ means _____.

Write the three root letters of הַקָּדוֹשׁ. _____ _____ _____

בָּרוּךְ means _____.

What is the root of בָּרוּךְ? _____ _____ _____

הוּא means "he." Because God is neither male nor female, we translate הוּא as "One."

READING PRACTICE

Fill in the word הוּא in each prayer line below. Then practice reading the sentences aloud.

1. מוֹדִים אֲנַחְנוּ לָךְ שָׁאַתָּה _____ יְיָ אֱלֹהֵינוּ.

2. עֹשֶׂה שָׁלוֹם בִּמְרוֹמָיו, _____ יַעֲשֶׂה שָׁלוֹם.

3. אֶחָד _____ אֱלֹהֵינוּ, _____ אָבִינוּ, _____ מַלְכֵּנוּ.

90

PRAYER RHYTHMS

We have studied the vocabulary of the first verse of שָׁלוֹם עֲלֵיכֶם.
Practice reading this verse again.

1. שָׁלוֹם עֲלֵיכֶם, מַלְאֲכֵי הַשָּׁרֵת, מַלְאֲכֵי עֶלְיוֹן,

2. מִמֶּלֶךְ מַלְכֵי הַמְּלָכִים, הַקָּדוֹשׁ בָּרוּךְ הוּא.

The remaining three verses of שָׁלוֹם עֲלֵיכֶם are identical to one another except
for the opening phrase, which varies slightly in each one. Read the opening phrases
of the three remaining verses.

3. צֵאתְכֶם לְשָׁלוֹם   2. בָּרְכוּנִי לְשָׁלוֹם   1. בּוֹאֲכֶם לְשָׁלוֹם

Write the word that repeats in all three phrases. _____

What does this word mean? _____

Look back at the English translation of the שָׁלוֹם עֲלֵיכֶם hymn on page 86. Explain
in your own words the theme—the main idea—of the song.

_____

_____

IN YOUR OWN WORDS

How can songs like שָׁלוֹם עֲלֵיכֶם and other זְמִירוֹת (Shabbat songs)
enhance a Shabbat family celebration?

_____

_____

THREE OPENING PHRASES

בּוֹאֲכֶם "come"

_____

Write the root letters of בּוֹאֲכֶם. ____ ____ ____

What does this root mean? _____

Circle the words meaning "come" in the phrases below.

בֹּאִי כַלָּה, בֹּאִי כַלָּה:

Do you recognize the prayer in which these phrases appear?

Write the name here. _____ *(Hint: See page 68 in this book.)*

בָּרְכוּנִי "bless me"

_____

Write the root letters of בָּרְכוּנִי. ____ ____ ____

What does this root mean? _____

The word ending (suffix) ִי means "me" or "my."
Circle the word ending in each word below.

וְגוֹאֲלִי צוּרִי פִּי נַפְשִׁי לִבִּי לְשׁוֹנִי בִּי שֶׁעָשַׂנִי

צֵאתְכֶם "depart"

_____

The root of צֵאתְכֶם is יצא. (In some words the י does not appear.)

The root יצא tells us that "depart" or "go out" is part of a word's meaning.

Look back at page 86 and read the three phrases that begin with the words you just learned: צֵאתְכֶם, בָּרְכוּנִי, and בּוֹאֲכֶם.

THE HOLIDAY CONNECTION

Words with the root יצא ("depart," "leave") occur over and over again in the Passover Haggadah. The phrase יְצִיאַת מִצְרַיִם means "Exodus from Egypt."

Why do you think words built on the root יצא occur so frequently in the Passover story?

___

Read each line from the הַגָּדָה below and circle the word with the root יצא.

(Remember: Sometimes the י does not appear.)

1. בְּצֵאת יִשְׂרָאֵל מִמִּצְרָיִם בֵּית יַעֲקֹב מֵעַם לֹעֵז.

2. וַיּוֹצִיאֵנוּ יְיָ אֱלֹהֵינוּ מִשָּׁם בְּיָד חֲזָקָה וּבִזְרֹעַ נְטוּיָה.

3. אִלּוּ הוֹצִיאָנוּ מִמִּצְרַיִם, וְלֹא עָשָׂה בָהֶם שְׁפָטִים, דַּיֵּנוּ.

4. בְּכָל דּוֹר וָדוֹר חַיָּב אָדָם לִרְאוֹת אֶת־עַצְמוֹ כְּאִלּוּ הוּא יָצָא מִמִּצְרָיִם.

5. בַּעֲבוּר זֶה עָשָׂה יְיָ לִי בְּצֵאתִי מִמִּצְרָיִם.

The Passover Haggadah tells the story of our people's exodus from slavery in Egypt.

93

An Ethical Echo

Each Friday, before lighting Shabbat candles, it is a tradition to put money into a tzedakah box. The word צְדָקָה comes from the same root as the word צֶדֶק, meaning "justice." Jewish tradition does not rely on kind impulses alone to make sure we help the hungry, the homeless, and the needy. Instead it tells us we *must* take care of the needy—it is a mitzvah written in the Torah. Giving tzedakah is not just a nice thing to do, it's a commandment—an obligation.

Think About This!

How does giving צְדָקָה help us get into the spirit of Shabbat?

These two Israeli girls are collecting money to buy food for families in need.

During the Friday Evening Amidah, we say the following prayer, וַיְכֻלּוּ, which comes from בְּרֵאשִׁית—Genesis. The passage describes how God finished the work of Creation on the sixth day, then rested on the seventh day, blessing it and making it holy.

Practice reading וַיְכֻלּוּ.

1. וַיְכֻלּוּ הַשָּׁמַיִם וְהָאָרֶץ וְכָל־צְבָאָם. וַיְכַל אֱלֹהִים

2. בַּיּוֹם הַשְּׁבִיעִי מְלַאכְתּוֹ אֲשֶׁר עָשָׂה,

3. וַיִּשְׁבֹּת בַּיּוֹם הַשְּׁבִיעִי מִכָּל־מְלַאכְתּוֹ אֲשֶׁר עָשָׂה.

4. וַיְבָרֶךְ אֱלֹהִים אֶת־יוֹם הַשְּׁבִיעִי וַיְקַדֵּשׁ אֹתוֹ,

5. כִּי בוֹ שָׁבַת מִכָּל־מְלַאכְתּוֹ

6. אֲשֶׁר בָּרָא אֱלֹהִים לַעֲשׂוֹת.

מִלּוֹן

א	[illegible]	fathers
	אֲבוֹתֵינוּ	our fathers
	אָבִינוּ	our parent
	אַבְרָהָם	Abraham
	אֱלֹהֵי	God of
	אִמָּהוֹת	mothers
	אִמּוֹתֵינוּ	our mothers
	אָמֵן	Amen
	אֲנַחְנוּ	we
	אַתָּה	you (are)
ב	בֹּאִי	come
	בֶּאֱמֶת	in truth
	בּוֹאֲכֶם	come
	בְּנֵי	the children of
	בְּעֵינֶיךָ	in your eyes
	בְּרַחֲמִים	with compassion, mercy
	בְּרִית	covenant
	בָּרְכוּנִי	bless me
	בִּשְׁלוֹמֶךָ	with your peace
ג	גִּבּוֹר	might, powerful
	גָּדְלֶךָ	your greatness
ד	דּוֹדִי	my beloved
ה	הָאָרֶץ	the earth
	הַגִּבּוֹר	the mighty
	הַגָּדוֹל	the great
	הַקָּדוֹשׁ בָּרוּךְ הוּא	the Holy Blessed One
	הַשָּׁמַיִם	the heavens
ו	וְאַהֲבַת חֶסֶד	and a love of kindness
	וְאִמְרוּ	and say
	וְהַנּוֹרָא	and the awesome
	וְטוֹב	and may it be good
	וִיהַלְלוּ	(they) will praise
	וּמָגֵן	and shield
	וּמוֹשִׁיעַ	and rescuer
	וְעַל	and for, and on
	וְשָׁמְרוּ	and shall keep
ז	זָכוֹר	remember
ח	חַיִּים	life, the living
	חֵן	graciousness
	חֲסָדִים טוֹבִים	acts of loving-kindness
ט	טוֹבָה	goodness
י	יוֹם הַשְּׁבִיעִי	the seventh day
	יִמְלֹךְ	will rule
	יַעֲקֹב	Jacob
	יַעֲשֶׂה	(will) make
	יִצְחָק	Isaac
	יִשְׂרָאֵל	Israel
כ	כְּבוֹדוֹ	God's glory
	כָּל	all
	כַּלָּה	bride
	כֻּלָּנוּ כְּאֶחָד	all of us as one
ל	לֵאָה	Leah
	לְבָרֵךְ	to bless
	לְדוֹר וָדוֹר	from generation to generation
	לְדֹרֹתָם	for their generations
	לְהוֹדוֹת	to thank
	לְהוֹשִׁיעַ	to save
	לְכָה	go
	לְעוֹלָם	eternally
	לַעֲשׂוֹת	to make
מ	מוֹדִים	thank, give thanks
	מְחַיֵּה	give life
	מִי כָמוֹךָ	who is like you?
	מַלְאֲכֵי	angels of
	מֶלֶךְ	ruler
	מֶלֶךְ מַלְכֵי הַמְּלָכִים	Ruler of rulers
נ	נַגִּיד	we will tell
	נוֹדֶה	we will thank, give thanks
	נְקַבְּלָה	let us receive
	נְקַדֵּשׁ	let us sanctify
	נָתַתָּ	you gave
ע	עוֹזֵר	helper
	עוֹלָם	eternal
	עֶלְיוֹן	supreme
	עֲלֵיכֶם	upon you
	עָלֵינוּ	for us, on us
	עַמְּךָ	your people
	עֹשֶׂה	makes
פ	פְּנֵי	the face of
צ	צֵאתְכֶם	depart
ר	רָב	great
	רִבְקָה	Rebecca
	רָחֵל	Rachel
ש	שָׁבַת	rested
	שִׂים	grant, put
	שָׁלוֹם	peace
	שָׁמוֹר	keep
	שִׁמְךָ	your name
	שָׂרָה	Sarah
ת	תְּהִלָּתֶךָ	your praises
	תּוֹרַת חַיִּים	Torah of life